Circle Time for Adolescents

A Seven Session Programme for 14 - 16 Year Olds

Charlie Smith

Paul Chapman Publishing
A SAGE Publications Company
1 Oliver's Yard
55 City Road
London EC1Y 1SP

SAGE Publications Inc.
2455 Teller Road
Thousand Oaks, California 91320

SAGE Publications India Pvt Ltd
B-42, Panchsheel Enclave
Post Box 4109
New Delhi 110 017

Commissioning Editor: George Robinsson
Editorial team: Mel Maines, Wendy Ogden, Sarah Lynch
Illustrator: Michelle Maiden
Designer: Helen Weller

ISBN 978-1-904315-27-8

Printed on paper from sustainable resources
Printed in Great Britain by Cromwell Press Ltd

A note on the use of the words 'family' and 'parents'

Many children do not live in conventional two parent families. Some are looked after by the local authority and might have confusing and painful experiences. We often use the term 'carer' to identify the adults who look after such a child or young person. Sometimes 'people you live with' might be more appropriate than 'family'. These phrases can make the text rather repetitive. Please use the words most suitable for the young people you work with.

The worksheets

To photocopy the worksheets directly from this book, set your photocopier to enlarge by 125% and align the edge of the page to be copied against the leading edge of the copier glass (usually indicated by an arrow).

Contents

Chapter 1 Introduction and Background   7

What is Circle Time?   8

The philosophy of Circle Time   8

The aims of Circle Time   9

What Circle Time achieves   10

Skills developed through Circle Time   10

The link with self-esteem   10

The link with positive behaviour   12

The link with spiritual and moral development   13

The link with PSHE and Citizenship   14

Circle Time and the National Curriculum   16

The link with speaking and listening   16

Chapter 2 Circle Time with Adolescents   19

Supporting the development of 14 - 16 year olds   20

The 14 - 16 curriculum   20

Using Circle Time to support the transition to Key Stage 4   21

Circle Time delivery with 14 - 16 year olds   23

Chapter 3 Preparing for Circle Time in your School   25

Circle Time structure   26

Circle Time application   27

Working in groups   28

Setting up Circle Time   31

The role of the group facilitator   33

Rules   34

Encouraging active listening   36

Managing emotions   36

Managing behaviour   37

Chapter 4 Circle Time Techniques Explained   43

Chapter 5 A Circle Time Programme   57

Delivering the programme   58

Session 1: Setting the scene   60

Session 2: Co-operation   67

Session 3: Anger management and dealing with conflict   76

Session 4: Relationships and friendships   87

Session 5: Hopes and aspirations   92

Session 6: Stress and stress management   99

Session 7: Review, feedback and evaluation   106

Bibliography   112

The Worksheets

To photocopy the worksheets directly from this book, set your photocopier to enlarge by 125% and align the edge of the page to be copied against the leading edge of the copier glass (usually indicated by an arrow).

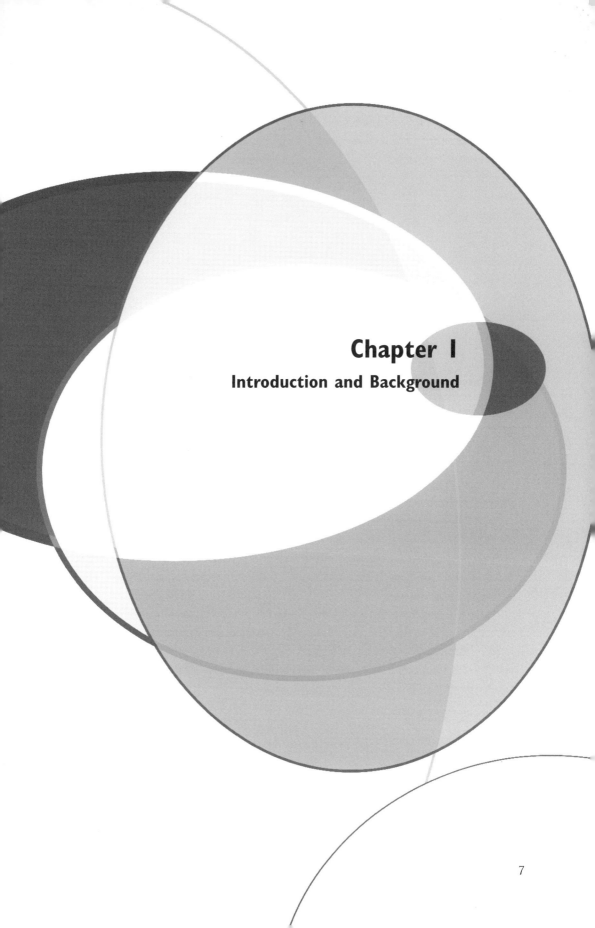

Chapter 1

Introduction and Background

What is Circle Time?

Circle Time is a structured, distinctive and creative form of group work, where pupils and the group facilitator sit together in a circle. Group meetings are held regularly; they create a safe, risk taking, trusting and non-blaming environment to speak, listen, share thoughts, explore ideas and interact. Circle Time is a way of supporting young people, raising their confidence and building their self-esteem; it is a tool to encourage them to believe that they are worthwhile people. Circle Time creates a caring group feeling where the people involved are valued and able to learn more about themselves.

Circle Time is not new to education; pupils from both the primary and secondary sector across the country undertake Circle Time as a regular feature of their timetable. Circle Time is increasingly popular in schools due to the impact of both its content and process in providing a distinctive approach to contributing, influencing and exploring communication skills and emotional, social and interpersonal development in pupils.

The philosophy of Circle Time

> "circle time is not therapy. It is not to be seen as treatment of any kind... we are not solving problems in a circle time session, but building skills of awareness. circle time is an educational model and belongs in a school curriculum along with other content areas. it requires no esoteric leader skills such as are required for counselling or doing therapy or treatment of any kind. no problem, in fact, is assumed. The teacher does not bring to the circle a 'something is wrong and needs fixing' problem mentality, and hence is not interested in analysing, probing or psychoanalysing kids...our experience is that people who simply pick up a book and start leading circles sometimes do so with the mistaken intention of doing some sort of problem-solving with students for instance, doing circles to 'reduce discipline problems'... It is designed to be done by teachers or facilitators with no special background other than a caring for children and an appreciation of the role of affective development in a child's experience."
>
> (Ballard, J. 1982 circlebook)

Current thinking around the concept of Circle Time was formalised by Ballard (1982) who identified ten value statements for its practice. Bliss et al (1995) in adopting Ballard's value statements identified a set of beliefs essential to the process and principles of Circle Time.

- Children are essentially good if they are treated with respect.

- Teachers are in a powerful position, responsible for the environment within which children learn.

- This environment should be supportive and accepting if it is to foster the best development of young people.

- Teachers should be thoughtful about the position of power in relation to pupils and should avoid using fear to control behaviour. Fear does not enable and it cannot encourage the development of self-motivated young people.

- Teacher's expectations of the ability and worth of a young person are inevitably transmitted and these expectations will affect the self-image of the young person. The teacher, therefore, has a responsibility to convey acceptance and encouragement.

- If young people are to become self-reliant adults they must be given the opportunity to make choices and to accept the responsibility for the consequences of those choices.

- The ability to make a good decision is dependent on knowledge of self and knowledge of others. In order to achieve this awareness, it is important to be able to identify the needs of self and the needs of the other person and to understand the conflict that may arise in a relationship where these needs are not congruent.

- Understanding of needs and resolution of conflicts depend upon two essential skills; the ability to listen when the other people speak and the ability to speak clearly about one's own feelings.

(Bliss, T., Robinson, G. and Maines, B. 1995, P5)

The aims of Circle Time

Circle Time has a host of aims bound in both its process and its content. However it can be described that Circle Time aims to develop the individualistic and unique potential of each person and develop and enhance their social, emotional and interpersonal growth. Ballard (1982) describes Circle Time based on achieving the three following functions:

1. Awareness – knowing who I am, the development of self and self-awareness.

2. Mastery – knowing what I can do, the development and enhancement of personal skills.

3. Social interaction – knowing how I function in the world of others, the development and enhanccment of social skills.

What Circle Time achieves

Circle Time gives young people the opportunity to:

- understand themselves and express their own individuality
- understand others and increase insight, awareness and sensitivity to others
- appreciate others and the value of friendships
- develop confidence and build self-esteem
- be aware of their feelings and handle them in a healthy way
- resist peer pressure and handle upsets
- enhance social skills such as co-operation, sharing, developing and promoting effective communication
- welcome new challenges and the opportunity to take risks
- promote self-direction and learn from mistakes
- look for alternative solutions and make decisions
- cope with change and difficulty
- develop conflict resolution and problem-solving strategies
- enjoy a full life
- have fun, receive affirmation and inject the 'feel-good' factor.

Skills developed through Circle Time

- concentration
- speaking
- assertion
- developing imagination and creativity
- turn-taking
- questioning techniques
- sensitivity and understanding
- friendships
- confidence and self-esteem
- group development
- giving and accepting compliments
- interpersonal development
- affirmation
- co-operation
- listening
- communication
- following instructions
- observation
- extended feelings vocabulary
- problem solving
- conflict resolution
- self-awareness
- mastery
- persistence and motivation
- empathy and compassion
- cognitive skills such as the ability to reflect, predict, question and evaluate.

The link with self-esteem

By self-esteem we refer to the evaluation that the individual makes and customarily maintains with regard to himself; it expresses an attitude of approval or disapproval and indicates the extent to which the individual believes himself to be capable, significant, successful and worthy. In short, self-esteem is personal judgement of worthiness that is expressed in the attitude the individual holds toward himself and the extent to which he accepts or approves of himself. (Coopersmith, 1967)

How much we like ourselves can be an overall judgement or it can relate to specific areas in our lives, i.e. we can have a high opinion of ourselves but dislike certain characteristics. Our self-esteem can be regarded as how we evaluate our self-image, i.e. how much we like the kind of person we think we are. Self-esteem will also be partly determined by how much our self-image differs from our ideal self (the kind of person – part or whole – we would like to be). The greater the gap between our self-image and our ideal self the lower our self-esteem. Low self-esteem could thus be described as disliking, judging or rejecting parts of yourself and high self-esteem as liking yourself for who you are.

In education, the issue of a child's self-esteem is a vitally important consideration. Self-esteem affects a child's behaviour in all aspects of school life including academic and social. Children with high positive regard are more likely to achieve academically and less likely to be in trouble than children with poor or low self-regard (Bliss, T. and Tetley, J. 1993). Children with low self-esteem look for information to confirm their poor view of themselves and behave in a manner which is consistent with this view. Examples of such behaviour traits include:

▶ fear of failure – finds it difficult to try new strategies or will simply refuse to 'have a go', will often destroy work even if it is good or avoid work and use delaying tactics

▶ feeling inadequate, useless, incompetent, unpopular and of little use – lacking in confidence and unsure of themselves, finding it difficult to make decisions, reluctant to join in

▶ appearing anxious or depressed – reluctant to join in, may become socially isolated

▶ rigidity in his or her thinking – negative self-talk about oneself, looks for proof of negatives, sets unrealistic goals for oneself that are either too high or too low

▶ feeling uncomfortable with praise – unable to or finds it hard to accept praise, feels unworthy of praise, feels that no-one likes them

▶ an inability to ask for needs to be met

- being disruptive – personal feelings of frustration and anger, attention seeking

- being critical and jealous of others

- an inability to be warm and affectionate – rarely laughs or smiles

- being negative about self, particularly in comparison with others – puts himself or herself down, negative self-talk.

Burt et al (1999) suggest that to value ourselves we need to feel some mastery over ourselves and to experience success. However, to get children with low self-esteem to 'hear' and believe positive messages about themselves can be a challenging task. They say that Circle Time aims to break into these feelings. In a gentle, subtle and safe way it can help young people to do this by building up personal and social skills and giving opportunities to experience success and praise and by affirming positive qualities.

Circle Time contributes to self-esteem through:

- devcloping skills and a feeling of competence (for example, expressing feelings, being assertive, communicating one's beliefs, contributing to decision-making)

- praising, accepting and encouraging individuals through their peers and facilitator

- being able to talk positively about oneself and celebrate achievements

- accepting that things go wrong sometimes and that it should not fundamentally impinge on self-worth

- providing opportunities to take risks and have a go

- receiving positive affirmation by peers and the facilitator and giving compliments to others

- emphasising a sense of equality, belonging, identity, security, trust and support.

The link with positive behaviour

"Circle Time's special strength is the effect it has on behaviour. Its value in training in human relations and interpersonal sensitivity is clear. Children learn to recognise how their emotions and actions are affected by others and how the emotions and actions of others affect them. They begin to learn new ways of looking at things, they are prepared to experiment with new behaviours and they have the opportunity to reflect on what these experiences mean for them."

(White, M. 1999 p21)

Circle Time has a large influence on behaviour through a range of avenues. Firstly, Circle Time has an impact on self-esteem and, as suggested earlier, low self-esteem has an influence over how we think, feel and behave. Therefore, it is sequential that Circle Time has a direct impact on how we conduct ourselves and how we respond to our own feelings. Secondly, the influence of our peer group plays an effective tool for facilitating change in our behaviour, values and attitudes. Circle Time provides an environment in which we can listen to and explore the views of our peers and thus as a result develop, shape or alter our own attitudes and behaviour. Thirdly, the content of Circle Time provides a social, emotional and interpersonal curriculum for young people, thus providing them directly with the opportunity to learn new behaviours and skills required for social and interpersonal interaction. Finally, the process of Circle Time, as we shall see later, provides a range of teaching methods that promote positive behaviours such as co-operation, turn-taking, listening and communicating. In summary, the ways in which behaviour is addressed via Circle Time are by:

- ▶ learning about oneself and relationships with others
- ▶ offering a non-blaming and safe atmosphere that offers a sense of belonging to a group
- ▶ peer influence
- ▶ acknowledging participants' views and feelings ensuring that everyone is valued
- ▶ the adoption of a facilitative rather than authoritative role where participants are in control
- ▶ discussing issues such as bullying, name-calling, aggression
- ▶ increasing awareness and the development of empathy
- ▶ the application of teaching techniques that enhance social skills development.

The Circle Time approach provides a tried and tested framework for the development of whole-school policy on self-esteem and positive behaviour. In 1989, The Elton Report (Discipline in School) was published by the government. It made many recommendations to schools regarding whole-school behaviour policies. The Circle Time approach can fully meet these recommendations.

The link with spiritual and moral development

The 1996 Education Act (Section 351) sets the National Curriculum within the context of the spiritual, moral, cultural, mental and physical development of pupils. The policy statement addresses these dimensions and seeks to identify opportunities that the school provides for the development of its pupils. The DfES Circular 1/94 similarly states that:

> "The Government is concerned that insufficient attention has been paid to the spiritual, moral and cultural aspects of pupil's development and would encourage schools to address how the curriculum and other activities might best contribute to this crucial dimension of education."

Spiritual development is about beliefs and values, the search for meaning and purpose, self-knowledge, relationships, creativity and feeling and emotions (Qualifications and Curriculum Authority, QCA, 1993). Moral development is concerned with human behaviour, especially the distinction between right and wrong and conventionally accepted standards of conduct. It is about ethics and conscience.

Circle Time offers an environment to explore and address these areas of pupil's development. With regards to spiritual development, Circle Time is a time when pupils can explore their feelings, values and attitudes and develop them based on the exploration of their own and others' views. Circle Time provides pupils with a safe environment to think about their own lives, share their experiences and listen to those of others as a means of forming opinions. Burt et al (1999) describes the connection between Circle Time and spiritual and moral development as a time where pupils can explore their 'inner life' (i.e. our personal attitudes, values and beliefs). They state that 'after we are able to explore our own inner self it is easier to try and understand the inner lives of others and the development of the skill of empathy'.

In relation to moral development Circle Time again provides an effective forum for development. For example:

▸ Circle Time rules are set by the young people and are adhered to in the circle

▸ activities used throughout the Circle Time process involve mutual respect and co-operation

▸ moral issues such as bullying, aggression, drugs can be discussed in the circle.

The link with PSHE and Citizenship

Personal, social and health education (PSHE) is a fairly recent addition to the curriculum in England. It gained high profile in the 1990s when the chief executive of the National Curriculum Council attempted to make it part of the state school curriculum. The Secretary of State for education has now decreed that Citizenship (now under the umbrella of PSHE) should be taught to all children from the ages of 3 to 16 years. From September 2002 Citizenship became a new statutory subject in its own right in all secondary schools.

Citizenship has three main strands:

1. Social and moral responsibility: pupils learn, from the beginning, self-confidence and socially and morally responsible behaviour, both in and beyond the classroom, towards those in authority and each other.

2. Community involvement: pupils learn how to become helpfully involved in the life and concerns of their neighbourhood and communities, including learning through community involvement and service.

3. Political literacy: pupils learn about the institutions, issues, problems and practices of our democracy and how citizens can make themselves effective in public life, locally, regionally and nationally, through skills as well as knowledge.   (DfES 2002)

PSHE covers the following areas of education:

▸ Personal education is mainly concerned with the emotional and psychological wellbeing of the individual. The promotion of self-esteem, regardless of whether this has to be developed by academic, sporting or genuine personal achievement.

▸ Social education is intended to develop collectivism and group thinking and prepare young people to engage with economic, social and cultural change. It should also equip pupils to make informed judgements.

▸ Health education covers not only eating habits and a healthy lifestyle, but also drug, sex and relationship education.

(Campaign for Real Education 2002).

The scope for Circle Time and PSHE and Citizenship links are wide. Not only can direct topics be the focus in Circle Time, for example peer pressure, friendships and relationships and drugs, but so also can many of the areas that PSHE and Citizenship education aim to address. These can be further enhanced through the Circle Time process itself. As previously mentioned Circle Time is a way of supporting young people, raising their confidence and building their self-esteem to encourage them to believe that they are worthwhile people. Circle Time aims to develop the individualistic and unique potential of each person and to develop and enhance his or her social, emotional and interpersonal growth. The process alone promotes the development of essential social skills from co-operation to communication.

Circle Time and the National Curriculum

Until children begin to feel positive about themselves, until good relationships are established and until there is a calm, safe, caring, well-ordered environment, the National Curriculum cannot be delivered effectively to all children (Mosley, 1993). Research suggests (Curry and Bromfield, 1994; Mosley, 1993) a high correlation between self-esteem and achievement; a child with low self-esteem is less likely to achieve their potential academically or socially than a child with good self-esteem. Thus by enhancing an individual's level of self-esteem one may raise their ability to achieve and, as noted earlier, Circle Time is an avenue for which this can be accomplished.

Establishing good relationships is also possible through Circle Time. Young people are not only taught new skills such as friendship, conflict resolution, being kind and caring, but the process also encourages the appreciation of others. As Bliss et al (1995) state:

"Circle Time is an inter-related, multi-layered process. Within the circle participants learn about self, learn about others and relate this knowledge to build relationships between individuals and between groups."

If one can create good relationships between pupils within the school environment and an ethos of caring amongst the school members, the foundations for creating a healthy learning environment are established.

Finally, as Mosley (1993) noted, creating a calm, safe, caring and well-ordered environment helps to ensure that the National Curriculum can be delivered effectively. Again these are aspects that can be promoted and reinforced through Circle Time. Through the establishment of pupil defined rules, co-operative activities, establishing a trusting and risk-taking environment and teaching methods that promote turn-taking, self-esteem, listening and respect, a positive learning environment is established which is transferred to the classroom.

The Circle Time techniques can also be applied within the classroom to teach the National Curriculum. Using the teaching methods of Circle Time (for example, sitting in a circle, rounds, free-think sessions) can impact on pupils' learning as well as have a positive effect over the social and behavioural environment within the classroom and between class members.

The link with speaking and listening

Jenny Mosley (1993), in her book *Turn Your School Around* describes how Circle Time fulfils the requirements of levels 1-3 for the statements of attainment in English. She notes aspects such as participation as speakers and listeners in group activities, responding to stories and poems, describing real or imagined events, listening attentively, responding appropriately to complex instructions and questioning and commenting.

Circle Time is essentially a speaking and listening process. Many of the Circle Time activities, teaching methods and games provide avenues for pupils to speak and listen individually, in pairs, in small groups or as a large group. Through Circle Time pupils learn how to communicate, how to speak confidently and coherently, how to actively listen to other people and how to respond to others verbally and non-verbally.

> "In Circle Time children can take part as speakers and listeners with increased confidence and be actively encouraged to comment constructively. Ideas and information are re-evaluated and logical argument can be practised…Circle Time is about positive communication and interaction."

(White, M. 1999 p20)

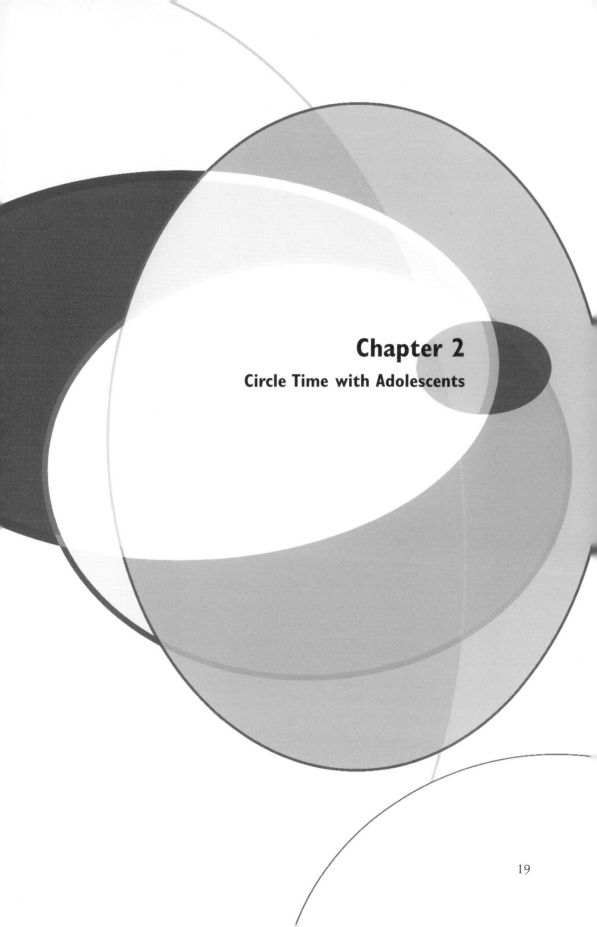

Chapter 2

Circle Time with Adolescents

Supporting the development of 14 - 16 year olds

Circle Time has predominantly been thought of as a primary school tool but in more recent times has been brought into Key Stage 3 in secondary education with great success. Circle Time with Key Stage 4 pupils is much less heard about and fewer resources exist to develop it with this age group. However when we think about the term development we reflect on the maturation process that we go through from infancy through to adulthood, not a process that stops as soon as we enter into adolescence. Throughout this process of change, of challenge, new experience and self-growth we often require (at some stage) the help of those around us to get us through the difficulties that life can throw at us. Circle Time can help young people to:

- understand themselves
- develop life skills
- welcome new challenges and the opportunity to take risks
- cope with change and difficulty
- promote self-direction
- enjoy a full life.

The conclusion is that through using Circle Time in Key Stage 4 – a time where one continues to develop through adolescence and into adulthood – we can influence the healthy development of young people.

The 14 - 16 curriculum

Taking a closer look at the curriculum for 14 - 16 year olds, in particular PSHE and Citizenship, Key Stage 4 pupils are already entering into a forum that has similarities with the content of Circle Time topics. It has been recognised in more recent years that adolescents require a curriculum that helps them to develop personal, social, health, moral and political knowledge and skills.

Personal, Social and Health Education is a fairly recent addition to the curriculum in England. It is a curriculum that enables pupils to clarify their own values. PSHE is about learning how to cope with the different things that you may encounter as you grow up and in your later life. Personal education is concerned with the emotional wellbeing of the individual; social education is intended to develop collectivism and group thinking; health education covers eating, healthy lifestyle and drug, sex and relationship education. In the National Healthy Schools Standard (NHSS), an initiative launched by the Department of Health and Education and Employment in 1999 to reduce health inequalities, promote social inclusion and raise educational achievement, it is recognised that schools need to:

- recognise that all aspects of school life have an impact on the personal and social development of pupils and that consistent messages need to be presented

- encourage pupils to recognise their achievements and do their best.

Similarly, from September 2002 The National Curriculum in England has included Citizenship, where there is a statutory requirement for secondary schools to offer a curriculum for Year 10 and 11 pupils based on providing pupils with the knowledge, skills and understanding to play an effective role in society. Chapter 1 talks about the aspects of Citizenship and the social, moral, community and political focus of learning for young people and again in relation to the National Healthy School Standard, the DfEE, 1999, state that:

> "The school needs to recognise that all aspects of school life can have an impact on the development of pupils in becoming informed, active and responsible citizens.
>
> The school needs to provide opportunities for pupils to be actively involved in the life of their school and communities."

If we reflect back on the contributions that Circle Time makes it is evident that it has a part to play in the curriculum of 14 - 16 year olds in school. All young people deserve the awareness, support and efforts of the adults around them to develop into fully rounded human beings with the strength and capacity to live a full and creative life (Danson et al, 1997) and educators are in a prime position to help, support and guide young people in their emotional, social and intellectual development.

Using Circle Time to support the transition to Key Stage 4

The transition between Key Stage 3 and Key Stage 4 is less well documented than that between Key Stages 2 and 3. After all, the move from Key Stage 3 to Key Stage 4 is normally made within the same school, unlike the Key Stage 2/3 transition, and is therefore seen to be less problematic. Statistically, however, there is a proven 'dip' in Years 8 and 9, particularly amongst boys. The in-between years of 8 and 9 are times when students can easily lose commitment to school. This 'dip' can be fuelled by many different factors that impinge on the young person as they move into Key Stage 4. They may feel stress from:

- their own and parental expectations of academic success

- changing friendship groups, which may alter as a result of different groupings for option choices

- peer pressure

- having to manage their own workload more than previously and meet deadlines for coursework

- having to acquire different skills in studying and revision techniques

- having to balance social and school lives

- the experiences of adolescence

- coping with the changing responsibilities and pressures outside school as well as in school.

Some young people make the transition well and experience few difficulties; others may need a great deal more support as they move into upper school and face its challenges and opportunities.

There is a need to prepare young people for the changes they will meet in Key Stage 4, as the following quote by the DES illustrates:

> "If change is to stimulate and not dishearten, it must be carefully prepared and not too sudden."

> (DES, 1967. para. 427)

Literature suggests that the current focus of this support is less pastoral and more on the continuity of curriculum and progress. However, young people moving from Key Stage 3 to 4 need to have their needs at transition met holistically, addressing emotional, as well as practical and educational needs.

Adapting to change is also dependent on a pupil's emotional state, their ability to establish social relations with peers and adults, their ability to satisfy their own needs within the environment and their response to endings in their previous year. They need to feel emotionally ready for school in order to meet new challenges with confidence (Goleman 1996). Children need to feel empowered at the start of the journey to Key Stage 4 otherwise they run the risk of not transferring well and developing problems caused by the stress of not settling into school (Fabian, 2002). The secondary school should consider how it can make the transfer between key stages as smooth as possible by trying to ensure that the young people's confidence and sense of wellbeing are protected. Pupils need to be empowered at the start of their journey to overcome anxieties and develop resilience that will give them a sense of mastery of their own lives (Fabian, 2002). Galton et al (1999) state that:

> "When pupils are prepared for making transitions, they gain self-confidence and are more likely to succeed. However, they also need to sustain an enthusiasm for learning, have confidence in themselves as learners and continue learning throughout the transition."

Circle Time with adolescents can help to prepare pupils for this transfer, 'build in' that confidence, support them emotionally and thus decrease the likelihood of pupils falling by the wayside at Key Stage 4. Through delivering Circle Time with this age group one can seek to provide a platform where pupils can:

- ▶ reflect on how far they have come and celebrate their successes so far

- ▶ talk about and look forward to the challenges of Key Stage 4

- ▶ develop specific skills for Key Stage 4 such as organisation, time management, stress management and study and revision skills

- ▶ find support for their emotional wellbeing at transition

- ▶ be provided with continuity of support between Key Stage 3 and 4.

Young people need sign posting, support, understanding, direction and confidence building at the start of their Key Stage 4 journey. Circle Time can provide a useful tool in doing just that!

Circle Time delivery with 14 - 16 year olds

Circle Time at Key Stage 4 is a more enhanced programme. It is developed for the maturity of older pupils with topics relating to the issues that they experience and leads on from other Circle Time programmes pupils may have gone through in Key Stage 2 or 3. Circle Time at Key Stage 4 can be used in a number of ways and different topics can be applied for use in different situations. For example, you may want to use Circle Time to enhance PSHE or Citizenship and the sessions can be delivered during these periods. The topics chosen in this book reflect some of the core themes of PSHE and Citizenship. Alternatively you may wish to use Circle Time with Year 10 pupils to help aid their transition into Key Stage 4. Through the delivery of Circle Time, either in small or class groups, you can develop both the skills and confidence of pupils and prepare them for the new and challenging experiences of Year 10 and 11, thus ensuring their successful transition. Finally you may want to introduce Circle Time into Key Stage 4 to enhance the development of pupils, encourage friendships, sustain a supportive, caring and listening school ethos or simply just to maintain a structure that your pupils are used to experiencing in all years of their education.

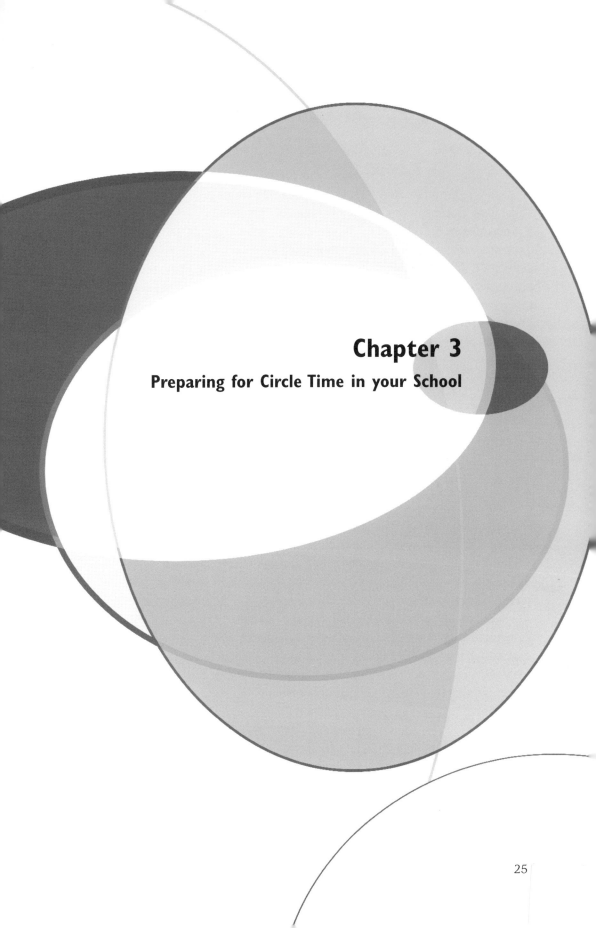

Chapter 3
Preparing for Circle Time in your School

Circle Time structure

In all group work there are stages of development. The Chrisyles Model of this talks of group work as having a beginning, middle and end.

The first phase

The first phase is a 'getting to know you' process. This is where procedures are clarified, ground rules are set and standards and expectations discussed. This initial process is very important as it sets out clear guidelines for all to follow and sets precedence for future good practice. Session 1 of any Circle Time programme needs to reflect this. Participants need to be engaged in activities that allow them to familiarise with each other and help them to bond as a group. The pupils need to establish their own set of ground rules in the first session. The facilitator also needs to ensure that the pupils understand why they are doing Circle Time and are clear about the aims of the programme. Opportunity must be provided in the first meeting for the pupils to voice their expectations. This initial process cannot be removed from a Circle Time programme; it is essential for its functioning.

> "Students can not directly express their own ideas and opinions until they have learned that their peers and the teacher will not reject them."
>
> Schmuck and Schmuck (1987)

The consolidation stage

The middle phase is about communicating with others through listening, verbal and non-verbal skills. Leadership roles and functions become more defined. Through co-operation and decision-making, the group members start to develop a trusting relationship and feel more able to talk freely and discuss feelings. As the group becomes more cohesive with time, conflicts become easier to resolve. These skills are learned through working together, learning to negotiate, respecting each other, being empathetic, expressing feelings and being assertive. The middle sessions of a Circle Time programme are specific topics that enhance personal and social skills. The Circle Time techniques or teaching methods are such that they allow for opportunities to communicate, listen, co-operate, make decisions and develop relationships with other group members.

The final stage

Finally, there is the ending, the tying up of loose ends and the summing up of how things have gone. The final session of any Circle Time programme needs to clarify the learning experiences of each individual. Time needs to be allocated to reflect on the process and content and the impacts that it has had. This helps the pupils to sustain the skills that they have learnt or developed and encourage them to use them in a range of life situations. An evaluation of the programme should be undertaken to help refine future practice. The final session, like the first, is an essential part of any Circle Time programme providing a closure for the participants and an avenue to say goodbye and well done.

In a similar vein, each lesson plan within the Circle Time programme is structured following the same format. Each lesson starts with an introduction, is followed by activities and finishes with a positive end thanking pupils for their participation and contributions.

Circle Time application

Circle Time can be applied in different ways:

- ▸ With a whole-school approach the Circle Time programme can be applied via small group work to a given year group. Here everyone in the year group has Circle Time built into their timetable for a set amount of weeks.

- ▸ With one-off groups the Circle Time programme can be used to raise self-esteem, build friendships and discuss current topics or to aid social development with a small group of children from a given year group.

- ▸ With class Circle Time the programme can be delivered with whole classes, curriculum groups or tutor groups. The programme can be delivered in its entirety as PSHE or simply help to gel a class and build rapport among the pupils and teacher. Sometimes class Circle Time is used as a means of induction to schools to help the pupils build new relationships.

- ▸ When teaching the Curriculum the Circle Time techniques can be used to deliver subject lessons. Here the teaching methods would be applied to deliver the syllabus. For example, the concept of multiplication might be the focus of the mathematics lesson. Sitting in a circle, the maths teacher may start by doing a round of simple multiplications whereby each pupil takes their turn to answer a question. Remember, the pupils have the option to pass if they wish. The next stage could involve a math game such as BUZZ. Here a number is chosen, for example, three. The pupils, one at a time, count from one upwards and when a multiplication of three is reached the pupil whose turn it is should say BUZZ rather than the number. A further idea may be using a tagline that has a two parts – one being an answer and one being a multiplication question. A pupil is chosen to start and reads their multiplication question. The pupil with the answer has to shout out, the response is then checked and the pupil reads their question out. This is repeated until everyone in the circle has read their question and shouted their answer.

For some subjects, for example science or English, topics from the Circle Time programme can be used directly if the school feels they match the syllabus.

Whatever method is used it is important that all staff in the school are aware of the process and aims of adopting Circle Time.

Working in groups

When people come together a set of 'group dynamics' begins to emerge.

> "Whether or not people take notice of group processes and the affecting factors in group situations, these factors do influence the outcome of group situations and often produce results that either in direction, intensity or nature have not been allowed for in the calculations of the planners. These kinds of consequence are frequently put down to 'human nature'."

> (Tom Douglas, Group Work Practice, 1983)

It is important that the Circle Time facilitator is not just an active participant but also an objective observer of the group dynamics. There can be an array of in-group processes at play within a given group. The following highlights aspects to be aware of and can be used as an analytical tool when working with groups of pupils.

Verbal communication

Patterns of communication and differences in the amount of participation of individual pupils may emerge in the group situation. Some pupils may dominate while others may consistently pass. It is the role of the facilitator to observe such patterns and adjust the lesson accordingly to ensure that all pupils participate on an equal and comfortable level.

Non-verbal communication

People's body language, gestures and facial expressions can tell you a lot about the way they feel, their attitude and persona. Picking up on participant's non-verbal language can help the facilitator in a group work situation.

Leadership and influence

The philosophy of Circle Time is that there is no 'formal' leader as such, in that everyone is equal. A facilitator for the group work however is necessary for Circle Time to function and the facilitator will need to be appointed from the start. The facilitator's role is not to exert their influence over the rest of the group but rather to guide the group through the Circle Time process. Pupil leaders may naturally emerge in the group who may or may not exert a strong influence over the rest of the participants. The people who speak most do not necessarily exert the most influence – total silence can sometimes give someone a high degree of influence.

Decision-making procedures

Whether we are aware of it or not, groups are making decisions all the time; some of them consciously and in reference to major tasks in hand; some of them without much awareness and in reference to group procedures or standards of operation. It is important to observe how decisions are made in the group in order to assess the appropriateness of the method of the matter being decided on and to see what effect the method of decision-making has on the group members.

Task behaviour

Certain kinds of behaviour are clearly aimed at getting the group task accomplished; we call this task behaviour. Examples for the facilitator to look out for in small and large group work include:

- ▶ initiation (asking for or making suggestions as to the best way to proceed)
- ▶ seeking and giving information (the sharing of facts, opinions, ideas)
- ▶ orientation (summarising what the group has done and keeping the group on task)
- ▶ clarifying (interpretation of new ideas, indicating alternatives and testing for agreement).

Maintenance behaviour

Just as important as task behaviour is the kind of behaviour which helps the group remain in good working order, creating a good climate for task work and good relationships which permit maximum use of member resource. Examples include:

- ▶ harmonising (reconciling disagreements and offering compromise)
- ▶ gate-keeping (helping others get into the discussion)
- ▶ encouraging (being friendly, warm and showing acceptance of other contributions through verbal and non-verbal behaviour).

Negative behaviour

In groups we sometimes see examples of negative behaviour, sometimes this can be useful and necessary, but often it is destructive. As a facilitator it is necessary to think about what the reasons may be for any negative behaviour that emerges and how it can be addressed within the group work setting. Some examples of dealing with negative behaviours are provided in the section titled 'Managing behaviour'.

Membership

For Circle Time to be successful it is important that each of the participants in the group feel that their peers and their teacher accept them. The degree of acceptance or inclusion in the group will determine how they behave, learn and participate in the group. Different patterns of interaction may develop in the group, which gives clues to the degree and kind of membership.

Feelings

Feelings are feelings, they simply happen. How we behave in response to our feelings, however, is a choice with an effect. When people come together and interact feelings are generated. Sometimes these feelings are obvious and are apparent in an individual's verbal or non-verbal behaviour. As a facilitator being able to read the feelings of the individuals in the group can be an important contributor to its success as a whole as well as for individuals. We can repeat exercises we know generate positive feelings and adapt exercises that cause negative feelings for any of the participants.

Norms

Standards or ground rules may develop in a group and control the behaviour of its members. Norms usually express the belief or desires of the majority of the group members as to what behaviour should or should not take place in the group. These norms may be clear to all members (explicit), known or sensed by only a few (implicit) or operating completely below the level of awareness. Some norms may help the group progress and some may hinder it.

This is not an all inclusive and definitive guide on what to look for when working with groups. It is a difficult task to be an active participant and an objective observer at the same time and it is easier to see the issues involved when watching other groups in operation. The pay-off comes when you are able to influence group dynamics for the benefit of all the individuals ensuring each member is valued and is an equal participant.

Setting up Circle Time

With all things there are always influencing factors at work. With group work there are a number of things that can affect effectiveness, cohesiveness and outcome. These include factors such as whether members are there by choice or not, why people have come to the group, what makes them want to come back every time, what people perceive to achieve from the group, what individual expectations are, whether the groups expectations are the same and whether the group know one another or not. These aspects need to be addressed in Session 1 as explained in the Circle Time structure.

Other influencing factors include how many people are in the group, how long the group is to last, the frequency of meetings, the make-up of the group, i.e. age, gender, religion, class, race and the environment. The checklist below outlines good practice in setting up Circle Time to help ensure the most effective process and successful outcome.

Room

It is important that the facilitator is allocated a room to undertake Circle Time. Using the library or hall creates difficulties and distractions. The room used needs to project a friendly and comfortable environment to create a safe place for Circle Time to be undertaken. Ideally, the same room needs to be used on a weekly basis to provide consistency.

Frequency and duration

The frequency and duration of sessions is governed by varying levels of concentration. The recommended time slot for secondary aged pupils is 45 minutes. This may vary depending on the group size and dynamics of the group. Consistency in sessions is important and it is suggested that they take place on a weekly basis. Sessions stretched over any length of time decrease the chances of pupils retaining the skills.

Seating arrangements

As one would expect from the title, the group work activity takes place in a circle formation. Chairs should be prearranged into a circle ready for the lesson. All barriers need to be removed, desks put to the side of the room and enough space created to allow movement of the pupils.

Using the technique of sitting in a circle creates a sense of unity, co-operation and equality; it indicates that everyone in the group, including the teacher, is equal; that there is no 'controller'. Circle seating ensures that everyone can be seen and heard; people can make eye contact, which is an important aspect of speaking and listening; the group is working together to support one another;

there are no physical barriers such as desks and chairs and everyone is valued as an important member of the group.

It is important to create a relaxed, comfortable atmosphere for the group. It is best to start by letting the pupils sit where they like in the circle. Rather than being prescriptive and authoritative the facilitator can then use games to get the group mixed up and to split friendship groups. It is important that the group facilitator sits in the circle with the pupils as an equal. This gives the pupils the message that the facilitator is not a controller but an equal member of the group, which is particularly important in developing an atmosphere of trust between teachers and children. It is also important that the facilitator is an active participant and joins in the activities.

Numbers

The number of pupils engaged in a Circle Time programme at any one time can vary considerably depending on the application chosen. For small group work the ideal size is about eight. Small groups help personalise individuals in the group and increase their sense of belonging and value to the group. Class Circle Time can be undertaken with larger numbers, the ideal size for larger groups is thirty; numbers that go over this are more difficult to manage. Very large groups can be time consuming; doing a round for example can involve a lot of waiting and very small groups do not provide enough peer support for pupils. Activities for large groups should be short and pupils encouraged to keep answers brief.

Pupils

Putting together a group for Circle Time is an essential process. Ideally the group should have a varied background of skills, be mixed in gender and be of the same year group. If there are targeted pupils in the group for behavioural needs numbers should be kept to a minimum so that negative or disruptive behaviours are challenged and positive role-models are prevalent to promote change. In cases such as these the suggestion is two targeted pupils to six role-model pupils. Pupils with behavioural difficulties often respond well to the Circle Time environment. They may feel more in control and have more individualised and positive attention. There are vast opportunities to raise self-esteem and help the pupils feel good about themselves. Pupils with emotional problems also benefit from Circle Time, the range of techniques applied to deliver the programme ensure that shy or withdrawn pupils are included. Circle Time can help develop confidence and a sense of self.

If pupils in the group have learning difficulties there may be a need to differentiate the work for them. This means that worksheets may need to be adapted, learning styles varied and more in-depth explanations given.

However, Circle Time is more active and oral than reading and writing, which means that pupils with learning difficulties will perhaps suffer fewer disadvantages in the learning styles than they might in the classroom. Pupils with other special education needs, such as visually impaired or hearing impaired pupils, can also be included into Circle Time groups as there is support in Circle Time from the teacher as well as peers. The work is of a co-operative, helping and caring nature. Be sure to know the make up of your group to account for their needs and to have the appropriate resources.

The role of the group facilitator

The Circle Time facilitator is the key to success of the programme. A teacher, a school based mentor or an external agency, for example an educational social worker, can adopt the role of the Circle Time facilitator. The role that the facilitator will play is very diverse; it involves organising sessions, times and venues, preparing work and resources, facilitating sessions and structuring the learning experience and responding to emotional issues. The Circle Time facilitator will be seen as a model for personal and social behaviours as well as attitudes, morals and values. Korfkamp (1997) outlines the 'musts' and 'shoulds' in relation to the role of a group facilitator:

The musts:

- ▶ The group facilitator must make each pupil feel important.
- ▶ The group facilitator must make each pupil feel valued.
- ▶ The group facilitator must make sure that each pupil is listened to and heard.
- ▶ The group facilitator must encourage participation.

The shoulds:

- ▶ The group facilitator should pay attention to what is going on in different groups.
- ▶ The group facilitator should always try to keep the pupils on task by every so often clarifying what needs to be done.
- ▶ The group facilitator should always try to encourage positive feedback.
- ▶ The group facilitator should always pay attention to individual pupils when necessary.
- ▶ The group facilitator should always allow the pupils to have the same opportunities.

The facilitator needs to participate actively in the process. The input will be most effective when it is seen by the children as a guide, not a judge, pointing out options without labelling them right or wrong, good or bad (White, 1999).

Rules

In all aspects of society we have rules. An analogy I often use with young people is through posing the question, "What would happen on a football pitch if there were no rules?" or, "If we didn't have any laws what might happen?" After this the pupils often agree that where people come together to work, to play or to socialise there are a set of rules in use. Sometimes these rules are written down, other times these rules are 'unwritten'; we behave or act in certain ways that we believe, based on our culture or value system, are most appropriate for the situation we are in and for the role we are taking.

Circle Time is flexible but, as with all successful structures, there needs to be some consensus of what is acceptable behaviour. Rules are important as they provide a framework within which relationships can develop and grow in a positive way (Curry and Bromfield, 1998).

It is important that the group has ownership over their rules. To do this the pupils as a group can free-think and record ideas for Circle Time rules onto a large piece of paper. They can negotiate priorities and select which they wish to use within the group. This way they will own the rules and therefore be much more likely to adhere to them. It also takes the pressure off the leader from being the law-enforcing authority.

Some rules that groups have evolved are:

- listen to one another
- talk one at a time
- respect the ideas and values of others
- keep personal comments positive
- opportunity to pass
- confidentiality.

Once the rules have been decided they can be displayed on the wall for the remainder of the group time together.

To ensure that the pupils follow their rules it is important to make clear to them that they are the ones to decide when someone is breaking a rule and what should happen as a result. For example, a pupil could be asked to leave the circle until they feel they can return and follow the rule. Whatever consequence is enforced, be sure that it is a consensus among the group as to whether an individual deserves it; this way the facilitator is not solely responsible for what happens in the group. Individuals making up the group can reflect on one another's behaviour based on the rules that they have decided to operate. This again places ownership on the rules and increases the likelihood of adhering to them. Be sure that the pupils, as well as the facilitator, openly acknowledge and praise one another for following the rules.

Two important aspects of Circle Time are confidentiality and passing.

Confidentiality

The contract between the pupils should include one of confidentiality. It is the role of the facilitator to ensure that the pupils understand the concept of confidentiality and apply it to the group situation. This can be an agreement that they will not discuss what the other pupils have talked about with anybody outside the group. This helps develop a climate of trust, setting an ethos where the pupils feel able to express themselves and take risks. It is important to explore confidentiality in the early stages of meeting the group you will be working with and to establish clear boundaries. A verbal contract should be made which the pupils and the facilitator can refer back to. The contract should state what both the pupils and the facilitator are aiming for – what can be expected as well as what cannot be provided.

In conjunction with child protection law, limits to what can be kept confidential will occur if someone discloses that they have been physically injured or abused, this includes:

- ▸ physical abuse
- ▸ emotional abuse
- ▸ sexual abuse (includes pregnancy)
- ▸ neglect.

Confidentiality of the facilitator may need to be broken if someone is experiencing severe emotional distress, if there are any concerns about the person's safety or welfare or if the facilitator has any doubts about their ability to assist the pupil.

The pass rule

It is important that the pupils engaging in Circle Time do not feel pressurised or uncomfortable participating. The range of Circle Time techniques allow for a variety of ways to engage the pupils, so for those that may not wish to speak in front of a large group they have the opportunity to undertake work in pairs, on worksheets or in small groups. It may be that at points in a Circle Time programme a pupil does not wish to participate and in this situation the pupil has the right to pass. At the end of the activity it is important to return to the pupil and allow them the opportunity to answer, contribute or comment if they wish to.

Encouraging active listening

As previously noted, Circle Time is essentially a speaking and listening process. Many of the Circle Time activities, teaching methods and games involve the skill of active listening, a skill that involves offering our full attention to another. Curry and Bromfield (1998) identify ten components of active listening:

1. Having eye contact with the person who is talking.

2. Giving full attention.

3. Sitting quietly without distracting the person who is talking.

4. Focusing on the speaker's needs.

5. Showing that you understand.

6. Letting the speaker express feelings without interruption or put-down.

7. Asking no questions.

8. Making no comments of your own.

9. Showing appropriate non-verbal behaviour.

10. Communicating acceptance no matter what the speaker is saying.

It is important that the facilitator also actively listens to the group members. Based on what is disclosed, discussed, what values or attitudes emerge and what feelings are expressed it is not the role of the facilitator to give advice, make comments or judgements, provide sympathy or solutions, agree, disagree, argue, praise or blame. The role of the facilitator is to model Circle Time behaviour, they are to simply listen to and accept individuals, to take a neutral role. Active listening is important to provide an atmosphere of co-operation, trust, acceptance and mutual regard.

It is important that the facilitator encourages the pupils in the group to actively listen to one another. This can be done through establishing rules, playing listening games, using a talking object and adopting appropriate techniques that encourage listening (see Chapter 4: Circle Time Techniques Explained).

Managing emotions

Within the group situation the pupils may experience a range of both positive and negative emotions (strong feelings). It is important that the facilitator is able to deal with the pupils' emotions. As noted earlier, sometimes feelings are obvious and are apparent in an individual's verbal or non-verbal behaviour. As a facilitator, being able to read the feelings of the individuals in the group can be an important contributor to its success as a whole as well as for individuals within it. According to White (1999) the Circle Time facilitator needs to have a 'personal warmth' demonstrated by a good vocabulary of feelings and a sensitivity to emotional needs, the facilitator also needs to be comfortable in dealing with emotional issues.

When we are presented with strong feelings or information that is painful it is natural to feel that we need to respond; we do not have to, it is not the role of the facilitator to be a therapist or to provide solutions. Listening, understanding and accepting are usually enough. As Bliss et al (1995) state, 'The process is intended to help an individual to be aware of her feelings and learn ways to express feelings in a safe environment.'

Follow-ups

It is important that if information is disclosed that either falls within the realms of child protection, if the pupil appears to be experiencing severe emotional distress or if there are any concerns about the person's safety or welfare that the facilitator conducts a follow-up session with the pupil. The follow-up session may be undertaken with the facilitator or the facilitator with a person who is more experienced in handling such situations. If a pupil makes a disclosure within a group situation it is appropriate to acknowledge it by saying something along the lines of, "That seems like something you can talk to me about when the group has finished, could you stay and talk to me at the end?"

Circle Time helps to enhance self-esteem and confidence, thus pupils with emotional problems benefit immensely from engaging in group work of this nature. The facilitator needs to ensure that a positive ethos develops within the group, that there are ample opportunities for affirmation, positive self-review and praise and that a range of activities are included to promote this.

Managing behaviour

As noted earlier, within group situations negative behaviours may arise. It is important that pupils with behaviour problems are not simply excluded from group work such as Circle Time as much of the time this type of support helps to challenge and change behaviour patterns. Increasing the self-esteem of pupils so they feel better about themselves can have huge impacts on behaviour. To help avoid behaviour incidents in the group, and address them if they should arise, the checklist below describes a number of strategies and forward planning principles that can be of use to the facilitator.

Gaining quiet

Circle Time involves playing games and games can become very noisy. Groups can also become noisy on their own; for these reasons it is important for the facilitator and the participants to agree a signal that indicates the need for quiet. This can be a clap of the hands, the blow of a whistle or a bang on the wall. Inform the pupils that any time they hear this signal they need to return to their seats and stop talking. If the group finds this difficult make this a fun exercise, i.e. the first person gets a prize and the last person has to play a simple (but fun) forfeit.

Clear rules and expectations

Ensure that a set of group rules has been devised, that they are clear, that pupils understand them and that they are displayed. Try and phrase the rules positively stating the behaviour that you want. For example, rather than the rule 'don't all talk at once' state the rule as 'one person to talk at a time; raise your hand to signal to talk'. Make sure that any new rules that are introduced into the group, i.e. rules for a game that is to be played, are given clearly and concisely. Use the rules to praise pupils when they are good, offer negative consequences as a choice. Ensure that when dealing with a negative situation you label the act and not the child, for example, "I like you but I don't like it when you choose to interrupt other people," rather than, "You are a rude person."

Opportunities for praise

Catch the pupils being good. Even difficult pupils are good sometimes, be sure to praise them if they are doing the right things. Most people watch for negative behaviour. Use at least three times as many praise statements as negative ones. Try to start and finish every Circle Time session with a positive. Start every session with a clean slate – give everyone a chance to choose positive consequences first.

Forward planning

Don't arrive for Circle Time at the same time as the pupils; you will need to forward plan. Make sure the room is ready, materials are prepared, their work is displayed on the wall, the rules are up and so forth. Ensure that you know the lesson plan, make sure that the activities in the lesson plan fit the group that you are working with and keep the lesson clear, interesting and moving at a brisk pace.

Use incentives

The use of games in Circle Time is an excellent incentive for pupils. Games can be used as an incentive for finishing an activity. Other incentives may be personalised to the individuals in the group.

Have a sense of humour

By integrating your own sense of humour, sharing yourself with the pupils and being an active part of the group you will help bridge a relationship with the pupils. The impact of this on behaviour is enormous.

Look for causes of problems

Analyse any problems after the session. It is important to ask yourself why the problem occurred and what the source of the problem may be. Sometimes there is a simple solution that can be acted on. It may be that a follow-up session is needed with a pupil or pupils who are causing particular difficulties. You could set an individual target for the group to help them to stay focused and on task.

Promote pupil responsibility

To encourage pupils to take responsibility allow them to:

▶ prepare the rules as a group
▶ decide on consequences (positive and negative)
▶ choose games
▶ contribute
▶ take on different responsibilities (i.e. peer tutoring).

Ensure that the pupils are offered choices and that they are in control of their participation. Pupil responsibility is empowering and allows them to develop their own learning environment.

Facilitator behaviour

Ensure that you are a model for the pupils by:

▶ being confident in your approach
▶ showing good non-verbal communication
▶ using positive and clear language
▶ having a positive belief and attitude
▶ building relationships with the pupils.

The behaviour of the facilitator, the language they use and the choices they make can have a profound impact on the pupils and the success of the group.

Use games

Games are an excellent tool in Circle Time. If you feel that the group needs a legitimate reason to move, needs a boost of energy, needs to laugh or inappropriate pairings or groups need to be split up simply play a game. Have a bank of games in reserve that you can call on. Games mix pupils, achieve quiet and help refocus; use them to your advantage.

Change Seats

Aims: Mixing, legitimate movement, fun

Resources: None

What to do: Based on a theme (for example, cars, desserts, fruit, countries) choose four categories (for example, for cars it could be Mini, Escort, BMW, Ferrari). Going around the circle, label the pupils in turn based on your four categories. Explain that when you call out a category those who have been labelled as that category are to get up and change places. When you call out the phrase (i.e. motorway, dessert tray, fruit basket, globe – an imaginative phase that encapsulates all of the categories) they should all get up and change places.

Chinese Fingers

Aims: Concentration, fun

Resources: None

What to do: Sitting in the circle, the pupils face the back of the person sitting on their left. A pupil is chosen to start and they draw a simple shape or a number on the back of the person they are looking at. This pupil then copies the shape or number they think was drawn onto their back onto the back of the pupil they are facing. This continues around the circle until it reaches the last person in the circle who states the number or shape they believe was drawn on their back.

Copy the Leader

Aims: Concentration, fun

Resources: None

What to do: In the circle a leader is chosen who starts a simple movement. The pupils are to copy the movement. Once they have got the movement the leader adds another movement. This continues until the movements are too complex to remember. A variation on this is that prior to the leader being chosen one or two pupils are sent out of the room. When the leader has been decided they re-enter and their task is to guess which pupil is leading the group.

Balloons

Aims: Legitimate movement, fun

Resources: Balloons

What to do: You will need three to four blown up balloons for a small group and six to eight for a large group. The facilitator explains that the object of the game is to keep the balloons in the air at all times. Each person however must remain in their space in front of their chair, they can reach inwards, outwards or sideways to prevent the balloon from touching the floor.

Touch Down

Aims: Legitimate movement, concentration, balance, fun

Resources: None

What to do: Ask the pupils to form pairs. The facilitator calls out a number. The pupils' task is to have the equivalent number of points (feet, elbows, hands, knees) touching the floor. The last person to touch down with the right number of points is out; continue until there is a winner. The pupils can form groups of three, four of five to make the task more difficult.

Number Change

Aims: Legitimate movement, mixing pupils, fun

Resources: none

What to do: Number each pupil in the circle as well as the facilitator. The facilitator removes their chair and stands in the centre of the circle and calls out two numbers. The pupils who are those numbers have to get up and change seats. The facilitator aims to steal one of the vacant chairs to leave one of the pupils without a seat. The pupil standing now shouts out two further numbers, again they change seats. Continue until the group is mixed.

Simon Says

Aims: Communication, concentration, fun

Resources: None

What to do: The facilitator gives a range of instructions for pupils to follow, for example, "Put your hands on your head, touch your left knee, raise your right arm, point to the door, touch your nose." When the instruction is given with the sentence 'Simon says' in front of it the pupils should follow the direction, if it does not start with this sentence the pupils should not follow the instruction. When a pupil follows an instruction that didn't start with 'Simon says', they are out. Continue until you have a winner.

Ignore minor disruptions

Rather than focus on minor disruptions, direct your attention onto a pupil that is displaying the behaviour that you want to achieve in the group and make a clear positive statement. For example, if a pupil is fidgeting and you need them to be still turn your attention to a given pupil, use their name and say, "Thank you XXX you are sitting very still, that is what I need for this activity." By doing this you are not giving negative attention to a specific pupil, you are being clear about your expectations and you are catching pupils being good.

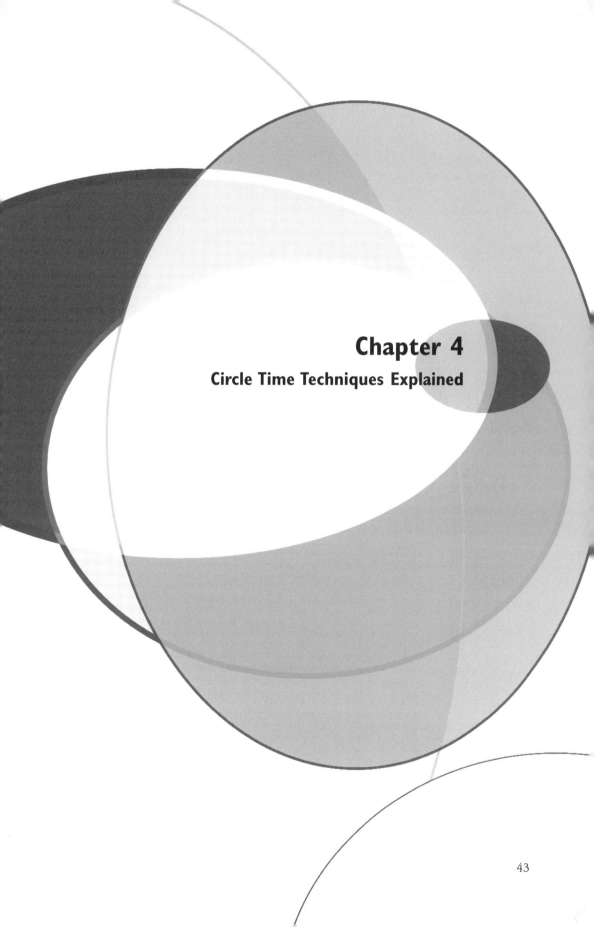

Chapter 4

Circle Time Techniques Explained

Games

Games are a core aspect of Circle Time and they serve a number of functions. Games can be used as a warm-up activity at the start of a session or a reuniting activity at the end of a session, they can be used as a tool to entice the pupils into wanting to continue the session and programme (particularly in the first session) and they can be used as an incentive to finish activities. Games can be used to enliven the proceedings after a heavy discussion period, to allow legitimate movement or as a method of refocusing the group. Games can be used to promote fun and laughter and bond the group. They can help the pupils to get into the pattern of working as a group co-operatively and respectfully.

Name games

At the start of a Circle Time course, games can be played to help participants familiarise with each other and remember each other's names. Name games can also be used through the course of the programme to create unique identities and individuality. For example, Charlie can be Cheerful, Happy, Articulate, Realistic, Lively, Intelligent and Energetic.

Mixing games

Games are a good way to help split inappropriate pairings and friendship groups. Naturally when the pupils come to the circle they will sit with who they are more familiar with or someone of the same gender. Games can be used to mix the pupils and change who they sit next to. By using a game to mix the pupils the facilitator is able to increase the range of pupils that an individual will work with throughout the course of the Circle Time programme. Separating peer groups, inappropriate groupings and friendships through games prevents the facilitator been viewed as authoritative or law enforcing.

Theme games

Games can also be used to initiate, promote and extend discussion on topics such as co-operation, listening and communication. By asking the pupils questions such as, "What skills were needed to play the game?", "How were the skills applied?", "What could be done better next time to make it work more effectively?", the facilitator can promote a discussion on a specific topic. Following games, further discussions can be created; the pupils can give examples of how they can use these skills in other areas of their life. Using games as a method of teaching is fun for the pupils and is an effective method to develop social skills.

The games are fun and useful and, if used correctly, can develop a variety of skills. Games can:

- diffuse tension
- break down pupil/teacher barriers
- improve group functioning and co-operation
- promote communication
- encourage creativity and lateral thinking
- enhance self-esteem
- enhance questioning techniques
- encourage instruction following.
- initiate group work skills
- build trust
- improve speaking and listening skills
- increase concentration
- stimulate thinking about behaviour
- encourage eye contact
- encourage turn taking

Rounds

A round is simply where the focus of attention is on one person at a time. It involves turn-taking by going around the circle in a clockwise or anti-clockwise direction. A round gives each group member the chance to make a contribution to the focus of discussion. One person starts, sometimes with an opening tag line such as, "I feel proud when…", "I am good at…", "The thing I care about most is…", or "Today I feel…" and the turn moves around the circle until everyone who wants to has had the opportunity to contribute. There are no right or wrong answers and no-one, not even the facilitator, is to comment or make judgement about what another person says. This helps the participants to take risks on voicing their opinions and ideas and feel at ease in expressing their views. It is also non-judgemental so all ideas are equally valued.

Using a round has a number of advantages. It allows everyone, including shy pupils and the facilitator, to contribute equally. It prevents the 'talkers' from domineering the discussion whilst allowing them to have a contribution and it gives the communication in the group a structure.

When using rounds there are a number of important points to remember. Firstly, one person is to speak at a time while everyone else is listening and secondly, there is an opportunity to 'pass'; this is important when discussing personal or sensitive issues. At the end of the round, the facilitator can ask those who passed if they now wish to speak.

Tag line rounds

A tag line round is when the facilitator structures a sentence that the pupils are to complete, for example:

"Something I did this week was…"

"I am a good friend because…"

"Co-operation means…"

Tag lines can be given verbally or they can be written down on card. Each pupil in the circle can complete the same tag line or can be given a different tag line on the same theme. Another method of using tag lines includes having a pile of tag cards that are turned face down and turned by pupils one at a time and completed.

Speaking rounds

A speaking round is simply where each pupil in the circle takes it in turns to make a contribution to the discussion. There are no prompts as such, just a focus for discussion and the pupils are free to comment openly, but in turn.

The talking object

To encourage the rule of only one person speaking at a time it is sometimes useful to have an object to pass around that indicates whose turn it is to speak. Only when a pupil is holding the object can they talk. The object can be passed around the circle during a round, or left in the centre of the circle for the pupils to pick up at any time they want to contribute. As a group, you could decide on a name for the object.

Writing rounds

Pieces of paper or worksheets can also be passed around the circle for the pupils to add their contributions to in turn. Or free-think sessions (described below) can be done in rounds.

Round games

Story telling whereby one person speaks and the next adds to the story continuing around the circle. Many games can also be played using this technique. Remembering games such as 'I went to the supermarket and I bought…' are also fun round games that promote specific skills.

If groups are too large, problems can occur with this technique when the pupils have to sit for a long period of time without activity other than active listening, for example, those at the start or the end of a round. In cases such as these, make rounds one word answers, for example, "Today I feel…happy, sad, angry," and elaborate on these after the round either in smaller groups or pairs. Alternatively the pupils can work in small groups or pairs to discuss the topic and then feedback in round style.

Curry and Bromfield (1994, 1998) suggest the techniques of 'double circles' for large groups. They suggest creating two circles of pupils, one facing inward and one facing outward, so that each pupil has a partner. A subject or tag line is then given for discussion and taking turns each pupil talks and then listens. After a set time the inner circle of pupils are asked to move one space to their right, so that everyone is now facing a new partner. The same subject can be discussed or a new one introduced.

Rounds can develop a variety of skills including:

- encouraging turn-taking
- speaking and listening skills
- enhancing self-esteem
- encouraging eye contact
- instruction following
- stimulating thinking about behaviour.

Free-thinking

One effective technique for gathering ideas about a specific issue, word or area or even suggestions for solution is free-thinking. A large piece of paper is placed centrally in the circle and each pupil is provided with a felt-tip pen. The facilitator writes a prompt, word or dilemma in the centre of the sheet of paper and then asks the pupils to record their ideas about the prompt. The pupils can simply write on the paper as they form ideas or the facilitator can ask them to raise their hand if they have an idea, so that recording the information is done in turns. Alternatively the facilitator can scribe as the pupils voice their ideas, or ideas can simply be aired without being recorded. During free-think sessions the pupils are asked to contribute ideas without commenting on anyone else's, all ideas are recorded and acknowledged. The technique should be non-judgemental with everybody's ideas being valued and accepted; comments about ideas should not be made. It is appropriate for the facilitator to add their ideas as an active participant in Circle Time. After the pupils have exhausted their suggestions, the list can be reviewed, categorised, simplified, placed in order of importance or discussed in more depth. Free-thinking produces a large number of ideas on a given area quickly; allows the participants to think creatively and contribute original ideas; involves everyone and shows that by working together more can be achieved – 'two heads are better than one' as the saying goes.

Tag free-thinking

The facilitator records a tag line for the pupils to complete in the centre of the paper, for example, "friendship is being there, caring, supporting, sharing, being honest, company, playing together."

Dilemma and solution free-thinking

The facilitator records a dilemma or problem in the centre of the paper and the pupils are to record a range of solutions, for example, "When Jamie first started school he didn't know anyone, what could he do?" Possible solutions are: join school clubs, ask for a mentor, introduce himself to people, ask if he can join in. Once all solutions have been recorded they can be discussed in more detail, categorised or rank ordered from most effective to least effective.

Word association and meaning free-thinking

The facilitator records a single word on the piece of paper and asks the pupils to think of other words that mean the same, then records short sentences about the word's meaning, for example, anger – mad, fury, hot, vexed, heart pounding, annoyed, something you feel, hitting.

Picture free-thinking

The facilitator should write a sentence, word or tag on the paper and the pupils have to cut out pictures from magazines that they feel represent this word and stick them on the paper. The opposite is that the facilitator puts a picture in the centre of the page and the pupils have to record things about it, for example, what they think is happening, how they feel about it or what the solutions or causes may be.

For very large groups free-thinking sessions can be done in smaller groups each having the same task or each having a different task. The same methods can be applied in these smaller groups and reporting back can look for common themes. Alternatively pieces of paper can be placed around the room at different workstations, each with a different free-thinking task related to a common topic. The pupils are split into small groups and rotated around the workstations; they are given a set amount of time at each of the workstations to record their ideas. The group is reconvened and the pupils are chosen or volunteer to report back.

Discussions

A discussion is an open forum where a topic is introduced to the group and guided by the facilitator using open questioning to prompt thinking. The pupils are free to make comments and contribute thoughts and opinions. Discussions, like free-thinking, give pupils the opportunity to share and express their views in a non-judgemental climate. It is important that rules such as turn-taking, listening, talking one at a time and respecting ideas and values, are adhered to during discussions. This ensures that the pupils feel valued and equal with everyone else and have the feeling that their contributions are necessary and will be heard. Discussions are a productive technique; they help the pupils to develop an awareness of oneself. Through making statements about what they believe in, who they are, how they feel and what they like they are able to learn about themselves as well as other people. Discussions give the pupils insight into the world of others, in that some people experience, think, feel or go through the same situations as them whilst others may experience the same incident but have different feelings, behaviour, outcomes and experiences. Discussions help the pupils to express themselves both verbally and non-verbally. Ballard (1982) indicates four ways in which Circle Time influences self-understanding and awareness, that are relevant to the discussion and many other Circle Time techniques:

1. Focusing on a particular topic or statement and understanding its implications.

2. Hearing other people's contributions and comparing them with our own perspectives.

3. Learning to disclose openly only what is comfortable to communicate at that time.

4. Receiving feedback by watching and listening to the responses of the group and learning from this feedback.

Discussions can take place with the whole group or the pupils can divide up into smaller groups and then report back to the circle. White (1999) stresses that discussions are more successful in small groups than larger ones and for this reason when working with larger groups, particularly whole classes, we should split them up. White talks about the importance of forming groups and that random allocation to grouping should be used rather than friendship. He suggests that this could be done through creative methods such as groups of the same hair colour, same month birthday, same number of letters in their name. White points out that the best psychological number of a group of this nature is three, a triad, and that sometimes it is more effective to bring two triads together for feedback prior to reforming the large group and taking comments.

Discussions can develop a variety of skills including:

- encouraging turn-taking
- speaking and listening
- debate
- interpretation
- commenting
- communication – verbal and non-verbal
- enhancing self-esteem
- encouraging eye contact
- self-awareness
- self-understanding
- encouraging the understanding of differences and acceptance of difference.

Worksheets

A worksheet in Circle Time allows differentiation in learning styles. Circle Time worksheets are usually kept very simple and do not take long to complete. Completion is usually individual but can be done in pairs or threes. Worksheets give the pupils the opportunity to express and reflect upon their own opinions, beliefs, inner feelings or thoughts on an area before listening to others in a group. Within a peer group situation, particularly when the group is new, the pupils are more likely to give their peer group answer and conform to the group norm when talking openly. Asking the pupils to complete a worksheet individually, prior to discussion further within the group situation, gives them a chance to express their individual response. Similarly some of the pupils in the group situation may not contribute verbally but will do so via written exercises; thus through varying the learning style it is possible to include all pupils actively in the process. Some individuals have not yet formed opinions or beliefs about specific areas and individual work allows them time to reflect on issues personally before listening to group responses. Both methods are important as noted by Ballard (1982) earlier, Circle Time allows pupils to disclose openly what they are comfortable with, develop self-understanding and hear other people's contributions and compare them to their own.

Reconvening the group and discussing worksheets is an integral part of the exercise as it allows the pupils to verbalise their opinions and listen to the views and opinions of others. When feeding back responses from worksheets it is important to express that there are no right or wrong answers and that if the pupils wish to pass they can. They may want to share certain parts of their worksheet or the facilitator may pose a series of open-ended questions to prompt further thought. Respecting one another's views is vital in this exercise so that each pupil feels valued and that their points, beliefs, feelings and opinions are valid even if they are different from others.

Worksheets are also useful as the pupils can take them away after the sessions and use them as a reminder.

Drama and role-play

Drama is where the group either creates or is given a situation with a sequence of events and a script to act out or perform. Role-play can be an activity in which a person imitates, consciously or unconsciously, a role uncharacteristic of himself or whereby a person remains in character to practise a series of skills and tries to implement them after learning them in theory.

Drama and role-play act as valid learning experiences especially for those who are visual and kinaesthetic learners. It is important, however, to be mindful of those pupils who find this technique difficult and uncomfortable and create other roles for them to play if necessary, for example, observer or director. Drama and role-plays can be used in a multitude of ways to help children to explore ideas, thoughts, feelings, solutions and consequences. They can be used to reinforce skills, practise them in a safe environment and generally allow the pupils to have a go at applying new skills.

By giving the pupils a character they are stepping into someone else's shoes. However, they can only express what they know; their thoughts, their feelings and their behaviour. Through using a character a safe environment is created for the pupils to express their views in front of their peer group. Also by introducing new ways in which their character can think, feel or behave we can encourage alternative thinking patterns without an individual feeling that they are being challenged directly.

Amongst other skills, drama and role-play enhances pupils' confidence, encourages creativity and imagination and promotes good communication.

Journals, diaries and think books

Curry and Bromfield (1994) introduce the ideas of using journals and think books in Circle Time. They say that some pupils find it too threatening to actually voice their thoughts and feelings and that by having an alternative method to record them, committing concerns and worries to paper provides an outlet for emotions, thoughts and anxieties that might otherwise be an unreleased burden. They suggest that the teacher can either record tag lines in the book or allow the pupils to record thoughts and feelings freely as a diary entry.

Giving all pupils in Circle Time a simple diary to take away is one means of self-monitoring. They can be asked to record specifics such as how they felt each time they became angry or the positive comments that they received during the week. Diaries are particularly useful in Circle Time when you are returning to a particular topic. They can be used as a tool to develop self-awareness and understanding. The pupils can bring their diaries to Circle Time sessions and talk about their entries with the group if they feel comfortable. Curry and Bromfield (1994) suggest that it may be useful for the facilitator to respond to diary entries by writing back or just acknowledging in some way that they understand the problem and that it is okay. For others their thoughts may need to remain their own and this privacy should be respected.

Poetry

Poetry can be used in different ways during Circle Time. The pupils can be asked to form short poems about topics such as bullying, friendship, hurt and so on. For some pupils expressing themselves through poetry is powerful, particularly for those pupils who are creative thinkers and rhythmical learners. Using poetry readings and asking the group or small groups to discuss content is a further way of using this teaching method or simply reading a poem to the large group to reinforce something.

Asking the pupils to read, listen to or write poems on a certain topic can aid:

- creativity
- expression of feelings
- literacy
- different learning styles
- expression of thoughts.

Stories

Story telling can be used to illustrate an issue under discussion, to prompt a discussion, to help form solutions or to promote speaking skills. The facilitator or pupils can read stories or extracts from books or magazines. Follow-up exercises can include discussing the thoughts, feelings and behaviours of the characters, and breaking the group into smaller groups and making up different endings to stories. If the story involves a 'problem' solutions can be free-thought by the group and the pupils can adopt characters from the story, discuss issues based on their character and examine consequences of actions. Stories can help to examine behaviours and feelings from different perspectives – individuals are very self-focused and usually see things from their reference point. Through using a story it is possible to examine the full range of people's views, options and feelings in a given situation enabling children to see different points of view. Stories allow for the topic to be looked at safely through the eyes of the characters, and using this technique (called 'one-step removed') the pupils can safely discuss their ideas through the characters.

Competitions, quizzes and dilemmas

The aim of Circle Time is not to create a competitive and hierarchical climate, however, engaging older children through setting them competitions, quizzes or dilemmas can be fun. Competitions and quizzes should not be between individuals but large teams where individuals can work co-operatively and interactively as a group. Competitions need not just be written work – for example, they can be about designing posters. Dilemmas can be given to the large group or small groups; here the pupils would be presented with a situation that requires them to work co-operatively together to find solutions to a problem. Competitions and quizzes allow the pupils to practise competitiveness and team opposition in an acceptable way. Dilemmas look at ways of problem-solving and aid co-operative working. Competitions, quizzes and dilemmas can be related to the focus of the session and they can make learning fun.

Debriefs

Debriefing is about providing more in-depth information after an activity has taken place. For example, the pupils may engage in a game, and initially they will simply see the game as a means of having fun. During a debrief after the game the facilitator can inform the pupils about the nature of the game, the skills that the pupils needed to apply to make it work and go on to create further discussions. Debriefs are an important aspect of many Circle Time techniques. The debrief is the way in which the children learn and put the theoretical and practical together. Debriefs help them to understand working practice, available choices and consequences. Debriefs allow time to examine individual perspectives and enable the formation of opinions.

Displays

During the course of the programme a number of posters will be created from the rules of free-thinking and small group work. Try to display these during the course of the programme. Displaying work reminds the pupils of the issues that they have addressed, demonstrates value for the work that has been completed and increases comfort, safety and co-operation as the pupils are surrounded by positive words and messages.

Folders

One optional suggestion is providing each pupil with a folder to keep copies of the work they complete during the course of the sessions as well as their Certificate of Completion. This encourages them to take away the skills that they have learnt and enables them to look back at what they have learned and how they have developed.

Certificates

Certificates provide a celebratory end to Circle Time; they affirm pupils' positive achievements throughout the course of the programme. Certificates can be personalised to highlight an individual's positive or special qualities demonstrated during the sessions. They can be presented by the facilitator, the head teacher or even in an assembly.

Certificates do not necessarily need to be limited to the end of Circle Time sessions; they can be given during the course of the programme for a whole range of things. Some ideas for certificates could include good listener, kind person, good work and most helpful. It is a good idea to tell the pupils how they can gain extra certificates and hand them out at the end of a session; the decision about who should receive a certificate should come from the group and not the facilitator.

Evaluations

It is important that at the end of a Circle Time programme an evaluation is undertaken. This can take the form of a round when everyone is asked to say what he or she enjoyed or did not enjoy about a particular activity, session or programme in general. It can take the form of a written evaluation sheet, picture association, face drawing or other creative methods. Evaluations give the facilitator instant feedback on the pupils' views of Circle Time and can be used to develop future sessions. They also provide an opportunity for the pupils to reflect on what they have learnt during the course of the programme and how they may have applied it to issues in their life. Furthermore, evaluations and reflection sessions enable clarification on areas that individuals may wish to expand; for this reason the evaluation needs to be a session in itself.

Chapter 5
A Circle Time Programme

Delivering the programme

The Circle Time for Adolescents programme comprises seven group work sessions that can be delivered to small groups or class groups. Session content on each of the topics provides adequate material for two separate sessions. The facilitator, depending on the requirements and nature of the group, can access a choice of material. Alternatively one longer session could be conducted or two shorter sessions. The content and format of the programme is again dependent on the group and the needs of pupils. It is the decision of the facilitator on the route and sequence of the programme. Where necessary adaptations to activities for varying group sizes are provided. Additional sessions to evolve the programme or extra activities to extend the sessions can be delivered if the school wishes to add to the package provided. Good practice on preparing to deliver the programme is outlined in Chapter 3 and should be read by the facilitator prior to delivery.

The manual takes the facilitator step-by-step clearly through each Circle Time session. The aims of each session are stated, lesson plans are provided and the resources that are required are included in the photocopiable pages at the end of each session. There is a register in Session 1 that can be used to record attendance at Circle Time. The sessions are highly interactive and are based on visual, auditory and kinaesthetic (VAK) learning and apply the range of Circle Time techniques discussed in Chapter 4.

Session 1: Setting the scene
Session 1 introduces the concept of Circle Time to pupils and outlines the content of the course. The purpose of this initial session is to create a safe, trusting and positive working environment. Much of the session is allocated to activities that allow pupils to get to know one another. Group rules are established and expectations are discussed.

Session 2: Co-operation
This session provides opportunities for pupils to learn skills of co-operation; the activities enhance social skills and reinforce group identity. The ideas of working democratically and solving problems together are explored.

Session 3: Anger management and dealing with conflict
Session 3 involves examining the types of situations that make us angry, recognising our physiological reactions to anger, examining the actions we may take in dealing with conflict (as a response to anger) and what strategies we may use in managing these.

Session 4: Relationships and friendships
This session aims to provide students with opportunities to explore their present values, opinions and feelings about different kinds of relationships, in

particular friendships. Students are helped to understand what friendship is and to recognise the qualities, which foster good relations. Aspects of relationships, those people with whom we have relationships both positive and negative and the importance of relationships, are also examined. The activities encourage students to apply what they have learnt.

Session 5: Hopes and aspirations
This session allows students to examine their future aims, hopes and aspirations within a realistic light. Students are encouraged to think about self-target setting, reaching and achieving goals, overcoming barriers and examining available networks in fulfilling such aspirations.

Session 6: Stress and stress management
This session explores stress and its management. Pupils will have the opportunity to identify their personal stressors in life. Through the identification of thoughts, feelings and behaviours related to stress pupils will go on to explore their personal coping strategies. The concept of relaxation and diary keeping will also be introduced to pupils.

Session 7: Review, feedback and evaluation
This final session looks at the skills that pupils have developed and learnt as a result of the Circle Time programme. It also aims to clarify any unanswered or unclear areas. Pupils receive a Certificate of Completion and fill out an evaluation form.

Session 1: Setting the scene

Resources

Register

A4 paper

Sentence Completion Cards

Index cards or blank scrap paper

Flip-chart paper and pens

Folders

Introduction

Introduce the session to the young people using the following information:

The purpose of the group is to discuss issues pupils may not usually get the opportunity to talk about within the school environment. In addition it provides pupils with an opportunity to develop and enhance their social skills.

The topics to be covered include:

- ▶ co-operation
- ▶ anger management and dealing with conflict
- ▶ relationships and friendships
- ▶ hopes and aspirations.

Sessions will last roughly an hour and will include playing games, having competitions, solving dilemmas and group and paired discussions.

Provide each pupil with a folder and explain that this is for the work that they complete throughout the course.

Ask the pupils to record their name on the register and place a tick by Session 1.

Activity 1

Name games
Go around the circle and ask each individual to state his or her name.

Provide each pupil with a piece of A4 paper and a pen. Ask them to write their name vertically down the left edge of the paper. Once they have done this they are to individually record a characteristic they feel is representative of them against each letter of their name. For example:

Chatty

Helpful

Articulate

Realistic

Lively

Inventive

Energetic.

When they have finished the pupils are to pass their completed poster to the person sitting on their left. Choose a pupil to start and ask them to introduce the person to the right of them using the information that they have about them on the poster. For the example above you might say, "This is Charlie. Charlie is a helpful, articulate person. She has a realistic outlook and she is also inventive and energetic." Continue around the circle until everyone has been introduced.

An alternative style introduction could be: one pupil starts off by saying their name and something they like or enjoy beginning with the same letter as their name, for example, "My name is Charlie and I like chocolate." The person to their left continues saying, "That's Charlie and she likes chocolate. I'm Thomas and I like theatre." Continue around the circle until everyone has had a turn. The whole group will need to co-operate by helping those at the end as it increases in difficulty.

Activity 2

Mixing game
The aim of this exercise is to get the group mixed up. Based on the following sentences ask pupils to:

Change places if you like pizza.

Change places if you have a pet at home.

Change places if your eyes are brown.

Change places if your birthday is in April, May, June or July.

Change places if you like watching or playing football.

Change places if you have a sister.

Allow the pupils to make their own 'change places if...' sentences up. Continue until they are sitting next to someone they may not usually sit next to.

Activity 3

Information sharing

Ask the pupils to form a pair with a person they are sitting next to (this should now be a person that they are not so familiar with) and label one person A and the other B. Explain that person A is to tell person B as much as they can about themselves, person B listens without speaking. They have two minutes to do this and they then change around. They should then decide on two or three things that they have in common. Once everyone has found commonalities each individual of the pair is to take it in turns to introduce their partner to the rest of the group and share one thing that they have in common.

Activity 4

Why are we here?

Create a discussion on why this particular group has been chosen to participate in the group work. The reasons are to:

- ▸ enhance PSHE
- ▸ develop Citizenship
- ▸ support transition
- ▸ develop new relationships in the year group
- ▸ provide them with a safe forum to discuss issues related to their age.

Ask the pupils what skills they think they will develop as a result of being involved in the group. They may be:

- ▸ trust
- ▸ co-operation
- ▸ communication
- ▸ listening
- ▸ social.

Activity 5

Rules of the group

Draw attention to the fact that every group requires rules in order for it to function. There are rules everywhere in society from sports to libraries.

As a group, free-think a list of rules that the group want to operate. Suggestions for rules could include:

- ▸ Speak one at a time.
- ▸ Talk politely and kindly to one another.
- ▸ Listen carefully.
- ▸ Respect one another's views, opinions and property.

- Everyone is allowed to have a say.
- There is a free choice to pass.
- Respect confidentiality.
- Have fun.

Once the group have made a number of suggestions take some time to discuss these and decide which ones the group wish to operate as the group rules for the rest of the sessions. Record the rules onto flip-chart paper and place them on display.

Activity 6

Sentence completion
Place the sentence completion cards in the centre of the circle and ask for a volunteer to start. The pupil starting is to select a card from the pile, read it aloud and finish the sentence on it. Once they have done so they are to pass the card to the person either on their left or right who also takes a turn completing the sentence. Continue to pass the card in the chosen direction until all of the pupils have had a turn at completing the sentence. Continue to work through the pile.

Sentence completions
"I'm happiest when…"

"I dislike…"

"I wish for…"

"The most important thing to me is…"

"I feel important when…"

"A perfect day for me would be…"

"I feel really special when…"

"If I won the lottery I would…"

"I'm proud of…"

"The best thing about being me is…"

Activity 7

Guess who and joke
Provide each pupil with an index card or a small piece of scrap paper and ask him or her to write a few things about themselves on it, followed by a joke (please keep them clean!). Fold the cards in half and place them in the centre of the circle. Ask for a volunteer to pick a card and read the description. Everyone in the group is to try and guess who the person is. Once they have guessed the joke can be read out. Continue until every card has been read out.

Activity 8

Round

Encourage each pupil to state one or two things that they would like to gain from the group, for example:

- ▸ know the members better
- ▸ control their anger
- ▸ have fun
- ▸ hear others' views on things.

Conclude session

End the session on a positive note. Thank the pupils for their teamwork, co-operation and kindness.

Register

Pupil name	Session 1	Session 2	Session 3	Session 4	Session 5	Session 6	Session 7

Sentence Completion Cards

Photocopy these cards and cut them into single sentences

"I'm happiest when..."

"I dislike..."

"I wish for..."

"The most important thing to me is..."

"I feel important when..."

"A perfect day for me would be..."

"I feel really special when..."

"If I won the lottery I would..."

"I'm proud of..."

"The best thing about being me is..."

Session 2: Co-operation

Resources

Flip-chart paper

Pre-prepared flip-charts

Co-operation Worksheets

Pens and pencils

Story Scenarios A and B

Prompt Card

Sentence Completion Cards

Introduction

Introduce the session to the young people using the following information:

The aim of this session is to help individuals learn the skills needed to co-operate with others.

The activities enhance social skills and reinforce group identity. The ideas of working democratically and solving problems together are explored.

Activity 1

Meaning

Prepare two pieces of flip-chart with the following questions:

What does co-operation mean?

What does unco-operative mean?

Present the pupils with the questions one at a time and ask them as a group to free-think ideas and write them on a piece of flip-chart paper. Take time as a group to discuss the ideas that they come up with and encourage participants to provide examples. Once the two questions have been worked on ask the pupils to reflect on the differences between co-operative and unco-operative behaviours, their impacts and their consequences.

Display co-operative and unco-operative sheets during session.

Activity 2

Co-operation worksheets

Individually complete the worksheets:

> ‣ Ways I do not co-operate with friends, family or staff at school and people I disagree with.
> ‣ Ways I co-operate with friends, family or staff at school and people I disagree with.

Allow the pupils ten minutes to think about their answers and complete their worksheets.

Reconvene the group to discuss. Using completed worksheets, ask the pupils to complete the following rounds:

"I have been unco-operative by..."

"I have been co-operative by..."

Activity 3

Problem-solving

The aim of this activity is to encourage co-operation between the group of pupils with whom you are working and allow them to practise the skill that they have been discussing during the session.

For small groups

Divide the group up into two and provide one group with Story Scenario A and the other with Story Scenario B.

For large groups

Divide the group into smaller groups of five or six; provide half of the groups with Story Scenario A and the other half with Story Scenario B

Present each group with the written story scenario and the Prompt Card. Explain that the pupils are to attempt to address the problem with every member of the group playing a part. In resolving the problem they need to work out:

> ‣ how they can address the problem
> ‣ what role each person involved will take and what they will do.

Allow pupils ten minutes to work through the problem. On reconvening the group allow each group in turn to present the problem with which they were posed. Each person must state his or her role in solving the problem.

The other group is to interrogate their solution or method of addressing the problem and judge how well they dealt with the problem as a team.

After the groups have presented their scenarios create a discussion about the co-operation and team dynamics that they observed in solving the scenarios. Use some of the following prompts:

- How did you behave in a small group?
- How did you feel others behaved?
- Was any one deliberately awkward?
- Who was the most helpful and why?
- How easy or difficult did you find the exercise?
- What roles did people adopt in the group?
- How well did you work as a team? Did everyone help?
- What group dynamics came into play?
- Did a leader emerge?
- Did someone make more suggestions?
- Did others simply listen?
- Did someone seek others' points of view?
- Did anyone clarify the list?
- Were there any conflicts?
- Why was this task relevant to the theme of co-operation?
- How did you help one another?
- What did you achieve working as a team and what impact did this have?

Activity 4

Sentence completion

Place the Sentence Completion Cards in the centre of the circle and ask for a volunteer to start. The pupil starting is to select a card from the pile, read it aloud and finish the sentence on it. Once they have done so they are to pass the card to the person either on their left or right who also takes a turn completing the sentence. Continue to pass the card in the chosen direction until all the pupils have had a turn at completing the sentence. Continue to work through the pile of cards.

Sentence completions

"When I need help I wish others would…"

"When we work together we need to…"

"I could help others by…"

"Working in a group is good because…"

"Today I would like to help a person…"

"Today I would like someone to help me to…"

"When I am excluded from a group I feel…"

"Dominating a group is…"

Conclude session

End the session on a positive note. Thank the pupils for their teamwork, co-operation and kindness.

Co-operation

Ways I do not co-operate with...

Friends

Family

Staff at school

People I disagree with

Co-operation

Ways I co-operate with...

Friends

Family

Staff at school

People I agree with

Story Scenarios

Story Scenario A

You are out taking an early evening walk along a coastal path to the nearby town. One of your group falls down a cliff and injures themselves.

Story Scenario B

You are walking through a national park when you hear cries for help. You can see an adult and a child trapped under a fallen tree, and one of them looks injured.

Prompt Card

Task

Given the problem you are posed with, as a group work out:

- how you can address the problem
- what role each of you will take and what you will do.

Reporting back

On reporting back you will be asked to:

- present the problem with which you were posed
- individually report back on your own roles in addressing and solving the problem

Other groups can interrogate your solution and judge how well you dealt with the problem as a team.

Sentence Completion Cards

Photocopy these cards and cut them into single sentences.

"When I need help I wish others would..."

"When we work together we need to..."

"I could help others by..."

"Working in a group is good because..."

"Today I would like to help a person..."

"Today I would like someone to help me to..."

"When I'm excluded from a group I feel..."

"Dominating a group is..."

Session 3: Anger management and dealing with conflict

Resources

Calming or Alarming worksheet

Scenario Cards

Pens and pencils

Pyramid of Peaceful Problem-solving handout

Introduction

Introduce the session to the young people using the following information:

This session involves examining the types of situations that make us angry, recognising our physiological reactions to anger, examining the actions we may take in dealing with conflict (as a result of anger) and what strategies we may use in managing these.

Activity 1

Open discussion

Create a group discussion using the following prompt questions:

What sorts of incidents have made you feel angry?

How do you feel when someone makes you angry?

What are your physical reactions to your anger?

What are the consequences of your anger?

How do other people react?

What do you do?

Encourage each pupil to provide examples.

Activity 2

Calming or Alarming responses

Hand out the Calming or Alarming worksheet, one per pupil. Ask the pupils to think of a time when they were angry and then using the worksheet decide which of the following responses are:

- ▸ Escalating (alarming) responses, responses that will make the parties involved angrier.

▸ Defusing (calming) responses, responses that are likely to calm the parties involved.

Reconvene the group to discuss similarities and differences in their thoughts.

Activity 3

Conflict scenarios

Explain to the pupils that conflict and anger are different, however, many of us in conflict situations experience feelings of anger. Research has shown that angry people in conflict situations are less likely to deal with a situation effectively or respond in a way that reduces the conflict. The aim of the activity is to investigate how pupils normally respond to conflict as well as the range of responses available to them.

Ask the pupils to form pairs and provide each pair with a conflict scenario from the selection available (try to ensure that the range of conflict scenarios are used). In their pairs the pupils are either to engage in a role-play using their scenario or talk through it with their partner. Whichever technique they decide the pupils are to try and work out:

▸ Who does the conflict involve?

▸ What is happening to cause the conflict – where are the points of disagreement?

▸ Why is the conflict happening – what is fuelling it?

▸ What does each person in the conflict want?

▸ What is likely to happen next in the scene?

▸ In what way may the conflict escalate?

▸ In what way may the conflict be defused successfully?

▸ What can each character do to resolve the conflict that is taking place between them?

Allow the pupils 10-15 minutes before reconvening the group for discussion. On reconvening the group allow each pair the opportunity to role-play or talk through their conflict to the rest of the group and discuss their answers to the above questions.

Based on these conflicts and the session so far create a group discussion using the following prompts:

▸ How typical are these incidents of conflict in your lives?

▸ What types of conflict do you find yourselves in and with whom?

- What techniques do you use to defuse conflicts?

- Which responses help resolve conflicts successfully?

Provide each pupil with the handout Pyramid of Peaceful Problem-solving. Talk through the negotiation procedure in relation to the conflict scenarios and other examples that the group have highlighted during the session. Discuss how it benefits all parties involved at the same time as defusing the conflict. Gather the pupils' thoughts and opinions on the process and how they may use it during their own conflicts.

Activity 4

Anger management
Re-emphasise the link between conflict and anger. Explain to the pupils that sometimes if we are able to control the intensity of our angry thoughts and feelings we may be better prepared to deal with situations of conflict. Pose the following question:

What effect does the feeling of anger have in conflict situations?

Ask the pupils to discuss any examples of their reactions when they were angry and engaged in a conflict.

As a group free-think ideas of the strategies people use to keep their anger under control. Discuss the effectiveness of their ideas and the short and long-term consequences of the techniques. Introduce the following ideas to pupils if they do not come up with them and again discuss the effectiveness of these:

- count to ten
- visualisation
- think positive
- self-talk
- walk away
- deep breaths
- say clearly what you want
- find out what the other person wants
- suggest solutions
- compromise when appropriate
- use your imagination
- channel the anger, for example, into sports
- change your environment
- use humour
- relaxation
- mediation
- traffic lights (red=stop, amber=think and green=go or act).

78

Activity 5

Sentence completion

Ask for a volunteer to complete the following sentence:

"Next time I feel angry I'm going to try..."

Going around the circle anti-clockwise ask each pupil in turn to complete the sentence.

Conclude session

End on a positive note. Thank the pupils for their honesty, hard work and suggestions.

Calming or alarming

Decide which responses are ones that are likely to escalate a situation, that is, make the people involved angrier and more likely to make the situation worse and which ones are likely to diffuse the situation, that is, calm people down and be more likely to help the situation get resolved.

Place your responses in order from the most likely to the least likely.

Escalating responses

Defusing responses

Sulk

Understand

Talk it over

Shake hands

Shout

Be assertive

Write a letter

Involve third person

Apologise

Joke

Hitting

Run away

Point blame

Gang up

Scenario Cards

Scene: School corridor

Tammy: "Why have you been saying those things about me? They really hurt and you know they're not true."

Liam: "Well you dumped me, what do I care how you feel?"

Tammy: "I really liked you but you're horrid to me.

Liam: "Well you dumped me and you made me look like an idiot and now I don't care what you think."

Think about:

> ‣ Who is involved?
> ‣ What is happening?
> ‣ Why is it happening?
> ‣ What does each person in the conflict want?
> ‣ What is likely to happen next?
> ‣ In what way may the conflict escalate?
> ‣ In what way may the conflict be defused?
> ‣ What can each character do to resolve the conflict?

Scenario Cards

Scene: At home

Hatty: "Mum, Mary is having a party tonight, can I go?"

Mum: "Yes, but be back at ten o'clock as you have school tomorrow."

Hatty: "Ten o'clock!! That's not fair everyone else can stay out later why can't I? It's not fair!"

Mum: "Ten o'clock or not at all."

Hatty: "I hate you, you're so unreasonable."

Think about:

▸ Who is involved?

▸ What is happening?

▸ Why is it happening?

▸ What does each person in the conflict want?

▸ What is likely to happen next?

▸ In what way may the conflict escalate?

▸ In what way may the conflict be defused?

▸ What can each character do to resolve the conflict?

Scenario Cards

Scene: In the shop

Matt: "Put this in your bag."

James: "No way, man."

Matt: "Go on you chicken. Do it!"

James: "No."

Matt: "Do it or you'll get it outside. Just slip it in your bag."

Think about:

▸ Who is involved?

▸ What is happening?

▸ Why is it happening?

▸ What does each person in the conflict want?

▸ What is likely to happen next?

▸ In what way may the conflict escalate?

▸ In what way may the conflict be defused?

▸ What can each character do to resolve the conflict?

Scenario Cards

Scene: In the school yard

John: "Oi! Dan, stay away from Becky."

Dan: "Why? She doesn't go out with you anymore."

John: "Just stay away from her or there will be trouble."

Dan: "Yeah, course. What are you going to do – hit me just for speaking to someone?"

Think about:

- ▸ Who is involved?
- ▸ What is happening?
- ▸ Why is it happening?
- ▸ What does each person in the conflict want?
- ▸ What is likely to happen next?
- ▸ In what way may the conflict escalate?
- ▸ In what way may the conflict be defused?
- ▸ What can each character do to resolve the conflict?

Scenario Cards

Scene: In the classroom

Natalie: "Why won't you talk to me? What have you been saying to everyone? They all blank me."

Suzie: "Just get lost you loser, no-one likes you and you're a stirrer."

Natalie: "Look, whatever you have said you're going to regret."

Suzie: "Yeah, yeah, all mouth and no action aren't you?"

Think about:

- ▸ Who is involved?
- ▸ What is happening?
- ▸ Why is it happening?
- ▸ What does each person in the conflict want?
- ▸ What is likely to happen next?
- ▸ In what way may the conflict escalate?
- ▸ In what way may the conflict be defused?
- ▸ What can each character do to resolve the conflict?

Pyramid of Peaceful Problem–solving

Give your views and reasons behind the problem.

Express what you feel and think that the other person wants and why.

Offer a range of possible realistic solutions to the problem that you could try.

Between you, choose the most appropriate solution; this may involve discussing the different options and how they would work.

Check that everyone involved in the conflict is happy with the solution and clear about what they are going to do to play a role in resolving it.

Conflict Resolved!

Session 4: Relationships and friendships

Resources

Flip-chart paper

Pens and pencils

Mate Market worksheet

I Don't Like People Who…Because… worksheet

Introduction

Introduce the session to the young people using the following information:

The session aims to provide students with opportunities to think about different kinds of relationships, in particular friendships, and to discuss their values, opinions and feelings. The session will help students to understand what friendship is and recognise the qualities that foster good relations. Different aspects of relationships are also examined, including the importance of relationships and the positive and negative relationships that we have with different people. The activities encourage students to then apply what they learn.

Activity I

Free-think

For small groups: Divide the group up into four equal groups.

For large groups: Divide the class into smaller groups of three or four.

In their groups pupils are to free-think the people with whom they have relationships and record their responses on to flip-chart paper, for example:

- ▸ friends
- ▸ mother, father or carer
- ▸ brother and sister
- ▸ neighbours
- ▸ teachers
- ▸ doctor
- ▸ dentist.

Ask each group to merge with another group of their choice. In the larger group pupils are to combine their ideas and then put these people into specific relationship groups, for example, friendship, working, acquaintance, family, professional, sporting.

Reconvene the whole group. Discuss the types of relationships there are. Briefly discuss the many groups of people we have relationships with in our lives, those we can choose and those we can't and why relationships are important. (Ideas to discuss could include: loneliness, working, getting on together, social life and making things work for us.)

Activity 2

The skills of relationships
Explain to the pupils that relationships are difficult, we have to work at them. They don't just happen and continue without effort from both sides. Create a discussion with the group using the following prompts:

▶ What common problems arise in the different relationships that you have?

disagreements	unequal balance of give and take
jealousy	conformity.

▶ What social situations are uncomfortable for people your age?

▶ What helps in uncomfortable situations with people?

▶ What are the skills you need to make relationships work?

listening	body language
trust	backing each other up
openness	small talk
honesty	tolerance
empathy	being able to forgive and forget
being supportive	give and take
not being critical	settling differences quickly
social grace and politeness	understanding one another
communication.	

Activity 3

A focus on friendship game
Ask the pupils to form a pair with somebody that they have not worked with before and provide each pair with the 'Mate Market' worksheet. Their task is to come up with a set of skills, qualities or positive characteristics that they would buy from the market if they were purchasing the best friendship they could buy. Each pair is to find a quality for each letter of the alphabet.

Reconvene the group and ask each pair to report back their most desirable quality, characteristic or skill of a friend.

An alternative friendship game could be: going around the circle in a clockwise direction starting at A and working through the alphabet each pupil is to name a skill, quality or positive characteristic that they would want in a friend.

Activity 4

People we don't get on with

Explain to the pupils that no matter how good we are at getting on with people, there will always be some people that we don't like, or that we have difficulty relating to. Sometimes we don't have the freedom to choose whom we work with and those we live with when we are growing up. We are going to investigate the types of people we have difficulty being with; we will then look at how to deal with these situations.

Provide each pupil with the 'I Don't Like People Who…Because…' worksheet. They should fill it in with at least five types of behaviour of people they don't like – not named people.

Reconvene the group and going round the circle in a clockwise direction ask the pupils to read out their worst sort of person from their list.

Create a discussion with the group about how to deal with behaviours that are annoying, uncomfortable or irritating. Use the following prompt:

- How do you manage to cope with behaviours in others that you find annoying, irritating or uncomfortable?

- How do you handle yourself in such situations?

- What skills would be useful to help you deal with such situations?

Activity 5

Poster competition

In their own time ask the pupils to design a poster that encourages positive relationships or promotes the qualities of friendships. If you can, award prizes for the best poster and ensure that they are used in and around the school to promote positive relations.

Conclude session

End the session on a positive note. Thank the pupils for their friendliness, contributions and ideas.

Mate Market

Record a set of skills, qualities or positive characteristics that you would buy from the market if you were looking for the best friendship you could buy. Find a quality for each letter of the alphabet.

A _____

B _____

C _____

D _____

E _____

F _____

G _____

H _____

I _____

J _____

K _____

L _____

M _____

N _____

O _____

P _____

Q _____

R _____

S _____

T _____

U _____

V _____

W _____

X _____

Y _____

Z _____

I don't like people who...because...

Record five types of behaviour that you find irritating, difficult, uncomfortable or annoying in people and why. Do not name specific people.

I don't like people who...

because...

I don't like people who...

because...

I don't like people who...

because...

I don't like people who...

because...

I don't like people who...

because...

Session 5: Hopes and aspirations

Resources

If I Had Three Wishes worksheet

Achieving My Wishes worksheet

Flip-chart paper and pens

S.M.A.R.T.(ER) handout

Sentence Completion Cards

Introduction

Introduce the session to the young people using the following information:

The purpose of this session is to allow the students to examine their future aims, hopes and aspirations within a realistic light. It will get them thinking about self-target setting, reaching and achieving goals, overcoming barriers and examining available networks in fulfilling such aspirations.

Activity 1

If I had three wishes

Individually pupils are to complete the 'If I Had Three Wishes' worksheet. Encourage them to include a description of the outcome of their wishes, how it may affect or change their life or the lives of others.

Reconvene the group. Going around the circle ask the students to read out one of their wishes and explain why it was chosen.

Activity 2

Achieving wishes

Individually pupils are to complete the 'Achieving My Wishes' worksheet. Encourage them to think about whether any of their wishes could realistically be fulfilled. Ask them what they could do themselves and what others may be able to do to help to achieve some of these wishes.

Reconvene the group. Going around the circle ask the students to explain how they will achieve the wish that they initially read out.

Activity 3

Eliciting help from others

Explain to the pupils that if we have a desire, wish, goal or aspiration we want to fulfil, we may request the help of others in accomplishing it. This may be in practical terms such as borrowing money or it may be emotional in that certain people can provide us with the confidence and encouragement to fulfil our desired goals.

Create a group discussion using the following prompts:

- Which people in our lives can help us achieve things?
- How do we elicit help from these people?
- What roles do these different people play in our lives?
- What can these people do to help us achieve goals?

Activity 4

Blocked aims

Split the group into smaller groups of three or four. Working as a group ask the pupils to free-think onto flip-chart paper ideas on what may prevent us from achieving our desired goals. These may include:

- money
- personal characteristics
- commitments
- resources
- time
- motivation
- parents, relatives or carers
- feelings.

Once they have come up with a list of barriers the pupils are to reflect on and discuss how they can overcome such barriers.

Reconvene the group and take any feedback that the pupils may have.

Activity 5

Personal aims

Talk about setting personal aims and self-targets, how they help us achieve goals and aspirations and the practical ways we may go about doing this. Introduce the pupils to the concept of SMART target setting. Provide them with the handout SMART(ER) Targets and talk through the aspects involved. Ask the pupils to think about one of their wishes on their original list and how they could apply the concept of SMART targets to help them achieve this, take some examples. Ask them to think about something that they would like to achieve by next week. Going around the circle in a clockwise direction each pupil is to complete the following sentence:

"My aim for the next week is to...I am going to do this by..."

Activity 6

Sentence completion

Place the Sentence Completion Cards in the centre of the circle and ask for a volunteer to start. The pupil starting is to select a card from the pile, read it aloud and complete the sentence. Once they have done so they are to pass the card to the person either on their left or right who also takes a turn completing the sentence. Continue to pass the card in the chosen direction until every pupil has had a turn at completing the sentence. Continue to work through the pile.

Sentence completions

"One thing I have achieved is..."

"When I achieve something I feel..."

"I'd like to be..."

"I hope that one day..."

"I'd like to change..."

"I'd love to be able to..."

"My aim for this year is..."

"My aim for the future is..."

Conclude session

End the session on a positive note. Wish the pupils good luck in their personal achievements.

If I had three wishes

Record three wishes that you have and think about why you have chosen them.

Include a description of the outcome of your wishes, how it may affect or change your life and the lives of others.

Wish One

Wish Two

Wish Three

Achieving my wishes

Think about whether any of your wishes could realistically be fulfilled. Record what you or others may be able to do to help you to achieve your wishes.

Wish One

▶

▶

▶

Wish Two

▶

▶

▶

Wish Three

▶

▶

▶

S.M.A.R.T.(ER) targets

Small

> Make sure that the target that you set yourself is a small target; the smaller it is the more likely you are to achieve it. It is better to keep achieving small targets than to set yourself up to fail with one big one.

Measurable

> Set a measurable level against what you wish to achieve. This way you can tell if you have reached your target. But remember to keep it small and realistic.

Achievable

> Make sure that the target you have set yourself can be achieved with the resources, time and people that are available to you.

Realistic

> Set your target as something that you know is possible. We can set targets that become unrealistic; just make small realistic changes to steadily work towards your long-term change or dream.

Time limited

> When making a target, set out an estimated date by when you will achieve it. This way you won't keep putting it off.

Evaluate

> Check out your progress along the way; are you using the right methods to achieve your goal?

Review and revise

> Spend some time reflecting on how far you have come, if you seem stuck and are not moving towards your goal change the target slightly.

Sentence completion cards

Photocopy these cards and cut them into single sentences.

"One thing I have achieved is…"

"When I achieve something I feel…"

"I'd like to be…"

"I hope that one day…"

"I'd like to change…"

"I'd love to be able to…"

"My aim for this year is…"

"My aim for the future is…"

Session 6: Stress and stress management

Resources

Stressors, Reactions and Reducers worksheet

Flip-chart paper

Pens and pencils

Stress Diary example

Blank Stress Diary

Introduction

Introduce the session to the young people using the following information:

The aim of this session is to explore stress and its management. The session will look at what stress is and pupils will have the opportunity to identify their personal stressors in life. Through the identification of thoughts, feelings and behaviours related to stress pupils will go on to explore their personal coping strategies. The concept of relaxation and diary keeping will also be introduced to pupils.

Activity 1

What is stress?

As a group ask the pupils what the term 'stress' means to them. If necessary provide a few synonyms: anxiety, pressure, tension, worry, apprehension, burden.

Introduce the following information if it was not brought up:

- Stress can be healthy. It sometimes creates competitiveness, higher performance in people and improves how alert we are to situations.

- Too much stress when it is not dealt with well can cause problems. It can affect concentration, sleep, safety and appetite. It can also cause irritability, overreactions, self-blame, tearfulness, anxiety, depression and panic attacks. Being stressed over long periods of time can lead to physical and mental health problems.

- Stress has physiological signs; these include a faster heartbeat, tight muscles and being tense, headaches and a dry mouth, clammy hands and nervous twitches.

Activity 2

Personal stress triggers and reactions

Provide each student with the Stressors, Reactions and Reducers Worksheet
and ask them to complete columns 1 - 4 individually. Ask them to form pairs
or threes with other students that they feel comfortable sharing this
information with. Ask them to share one thing that stresses them and how
they think, feel and act.

Activity 3

Stress management

Split the group into smaller groups of four or five and ask them to free-think
the things that they do, have seen other people do or are aware of that help
them to cope with stress. Allow 10-15 minutes for groups to record their ideas
on to flip-chart paper.

Reconvene the group and take feedback from each of the smaller groups in
turn. Discuss which strategies would be helpful for different situations. If
students have examples and feel comfortable allow them to share these with
the group. Introduce the following stress management ideas if pupils do not
come up with them, again allow time to discuss them.

- Take three deep breaths and count to 10.

- Use visualisation to help you to stay calm or think of something or
  someone.

- Assert your rights, say, "No" to things. If you don't want to do them it's
  your right, but remember don't be rude or aggressive.

- Set yourself small and achievable targets.

- Reward yourself.

- Keep on top of things and don't let them pile up or put them off
  continually.

- Use self-talk.

- Use positive thinking.

- Don't criticise yourself. Someone once said to me, "Would you be friends
  with someone who spoke to you the way you speak to yourself?"

- Listen, empathise and try to understand other people's point of view.

- Show your feelings - talk to someone about what you are experiencing.

- Explore ways to solve the problem.

- Use humour.

- Make time to relax.

- Use muscle relaxation techniques.

- Take time for yourself.

Now that the pupils are more aware of the stress management techniques available to them ask them to individually complete column 5 on their Stressors, Reactions and Reducers worksheet. They should then return to their pairs or threes to discuss their strategy.

Activity 4

Relaxation exercise

Explain to the pupils that many types of relaxation exercises exist including stretching, breathing, visual imagery and meditation. Methods of relaxation fall into two broad categories:

- physiological relaxation techniques that involve the body systems associated with states of stress

- psychological relaxation techniques that involve a cognitive (thought) and behavioural process.

Inform the pupils that one of the most commonly taught and basic methods of relaxation is deep breathing. When a person gets angry or upset, changes in the body lead to an increase in heart rate, tense muscles and sweating. Deep breathing relaxation techniques can help to control breathing, heart rate and blood flow.

Explain to the pupils that you are going to take them through the deep breathing technique. Follow these steps:

1. Sit in a chair in a comfortable position. Arms and legs should be uncrossed. Hands should rest on the stomach and eyes should be closed.

2. Breathe in through your nose for a count of four, filling your stomach with air. Notice your stomach expand. Your chest should not expand.

3. Exhale the air slowly through your mouth for a count of six.

4. Continue to repeat step two and three about fifteen times.

Ask the pupils to open their eyes in their own time. Take some feedback from pupils about how they feel. Explain that when you are doing deep breathing for practice or for daily stress relief, you can do it for 10-15 minutes.

Activity 5

Stress Diary

A Stress Diary can be used to keep track of when you are stressed, the reactions you are having as a result of stress and also help you with techniques to apply to reduce the stress. Provide each pupil with an example and blank Stress Diary. Encourage the students to take these away and have a go at using them.

Conclude session

End the session on a positive note. Thank the students for their participation. Make sure that if any student would like to come back to you or talk to someone else further about stress they are aware of key people to contact.

Stressors, Reactions and Reducers

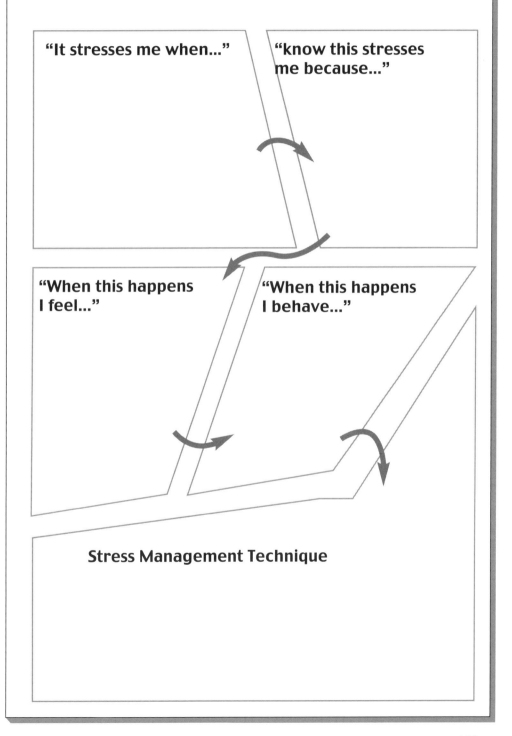

"It stresses me when..."

"know this stresses me because..."

"When this happens I feel..."

"When this happens I behave..."

Stress Management Technique

Stress Diary example

Name: Charlie Smith   Week Commencing: 1.9.03

Day	What Stressed Me?	How did I react?	Stress Management Technique:
Sunday	worried about PE on Monday	Got upset	Talked it through with my mum
Monday	PE	Tense and angry	I explained my worries to my PE teachers and felt much better
Tuesday	Nothing		I did some deep breathing this evening before tea
Wednesday	Too much homework	Ignored it	I realised I needed to set some targets to catch up with the backlog, I told myself, "I can do it and I will start this homework."
Thursday	PE	worried	I used self-talk. I remembered what my teacher had said on Monday and how nice she had been. I am also learning not to criticise myself
Friday	Nothing	Nothing	Nothing
Saturday	Nothing	Nothing	Went shopping and treated myself to a new top for addressing my worries in PE

This week I am pleased that I:

was able to talk to my teacher about how I felt about PE.

Next week I am going to try to:

get on top of my homework by drawing up a homework timetable and sticking to it.

My long-term goal is to:

Stop criticising my abilities and myself.

Stress Diary

Name: Week Commencing:

Day	What Stressed Me?	How did I react?	Stress Management Technique
Sunday			
Monday			
Tuesday			
Wednesday			
Thursday			
Friday			
Saturday			

This week I am pleased that I:

Next week I am going to try to:

My long-term goal is to:

Session 7: Review, feedback and evaluation

Resources

Sentence Completion Cards

Review sheets

Pupil folders

Pens and pencils

Certificate of Completion

Introduction

Introduce the session to the young people using the following information:

The aims of this session are to monitor individual progress, evaluate the learning outcomes and provide feedback on the effectiveness of the programme, course materials and strategies used.

Activity 1

Recap

Free-think and discuss the topics talked about over the last six sessions.

1. Getting to know one another

2. Co-operation

3. Anger Management and dealing with conflict

4. Relationships and friendships

5. Hopes and aspirations

6. Stress and stress management

Activity 2

Sentence completion

Place the Sentence Completion Cards in the centre of the circle and ask for a volunteer to start. The pupil starting is to select a card from the pile, read it aloud and complete the sentence. Once they have done so they are to pass the card to the person either on their left or right who also takes a turn completing the sentence. Continue to pass the card in the chosen direction until each pupil has had a turn at completing the sentence. Continue to work through the pile.

Sentence completions

"The most important thing I have learnt is…"

"One thing that has changed since I started the group work is…"

"One thing that I now realise is…"

"I liked this course because…"

"What I disliked about the group work was…"

"I am pleased I did…"

"I would like to do more of…"

Activity 3

How have we got on?
Hand out the Review sheets asking the pupils to complete them individually, comment as necessary then hand them back to you.

Activity 4

Group dynamics
Create a group discussion using the following prompts:

- ▸ How have we got on with one another?
- ▸ Do we feel that we know each other better now? What differences has this made?
- ▸ Do we have more contact with people in the group compared to before?
- ▸ What have we learnt about the importance of group work?
- ▸ What factors have enabled the group to work well together?

Activity 5

Open discussion
Give the pupils the opportunity to discuss topics related to feedback on the course. This may include topics still pending, clarification of certain components, suggestions for future group work, session content and so forth.

If applicable: judge the friendship poster competition and award prizes (see Session 4, Activity 5).

Activity 6

Presentation of Certificates

Present each pupil with a Circle Time Certificate of Completion together with his or her finalised folders.

Conclude session

End on a positive note. Tell the students that you have enjoyed working with them and have valued their contributions, ideas and hard work. Express that you hope that they will continue to apply the skills that they have learnt and developed.

Sentence Completion Cards

Photocopy these cards and cut them into single sentences.

"The most important thing I have learnt is…"

"One thing that has changed since I started the group work is…"

"One thing that I now realise is…"

"I liked this course because…"

"What I disliked about the group work was…"

"I am pleased I did…"

"I would like to do more of…"

Review

How useful has the group work been to you?

Extremely (1) (2) (3) (4) (5) Not at all

Did you enjoy the course?

Extremely (1) (2) (3) (4) (5) Not at all

Two things I disliked about the course

1	2

Two things I liked about the course

1	2

Rate the following

	Very useful	Useful	OK	Not useful	Of no use at all
Worksheets	◯	◯	◯	◯	◯
Discussion	◯	◯	◯	◯	◯
Teacher talking	◯	◯	◯	◯	◯
Role–plays	◯	◯	◯	◯	◯
Brainstorming	◯	◯	◯	◯	◯
Small group or paired work	◯	◯	◯	◯	◯

I would recommend the course to others (YES) (NO)

The most important things I have learnt are:

I would describe this course as:

◯ easy
◯ fun
◯ helpful
◯ irrelevant
◯ disappointing
◯ confusing
◯ stimulating
◯ entertaining
◯ interesting
◯ educational
◯ boring
◯ important

My suggestions for improving the course are:

Circle Time Certificate of Completion

Awarded to

For showing great co-operation and enthusiasm in attending the Circle Time sessions

At

Signed _____   Dated _____

Bibliography

Ashton, M. & Varga, L. (1993) *101 Games for Groups*, Pro-ed, Texas.

Ballard, J. (1982) *Circle Book*, Irvington, New York.

Barnard, M. E. & Cartwright, C. (1996) *Programme Achieve*, ASG, East Sussex.

Benson, P. L., Galbraith, J. & Espeland, P. (1998) *What Teens Need to Succeed*, Free Spirit, Minneapolis.

Bliss, T., Robinson, G. & Maines, B. (1995) *Developing Circle Time*, Lucky Duck Publishing Ltd., Bristol.

Bliss, T. & Tetley, J. (1993) *Circle Time a Resource Book for Infant, Junior and Secondary Schools*, Lucky Duck Publishing Ltd., Bristol.

Bond, T. (1986) *Games for Social and Life Skills*, Stanley Thornes, Cheltenham.

Britton, F. (2000) *Discovering Citizenship through Active Learning in the Community*, CSV Education for Citizenship, Essex.

Brown, J. & Fabry, L. (1999) *Overcoming Bullying*, Chalkface Project, Milton Keynes.

Burt, S., Davis, G., Lister, J., Morgan, R. & O'Shea, S. (1999) *Six Years of Circle Time*, Lucky Duck Publishing Ltd., Bristol.

Campaign for Real Education (2002) *What is Personal, Social and health Education?* CRE, York.

Collins (1979) *English Dictionary 21st Century Edition* Harper Collins, Aylesbury.

Collins, M. (2001) *Circle Time for the Very Young*, Lucky Duck Publishing Ltd., Bristol.

Coppersmith, S. (1967) *The Antecedents of Self-Esteem*, WH Freeman, San Francisco.

Curry, M. (2001) *Building a Peaceful School*, NASEN, Staffordshire.

Curry, M. & Bromfield, C. (1994) *Personal and Social Education for Primary Schools through Circle Time*, NASEN, Staffordshire.

Curry, M. & Bromfield, C. (1998) *Circle Time In-Service Training Manual*, NASEN, Staffordshire.

Danson, H., France-Jaswowska, A., Jefferies, B. & Weisselberg, A. (1997) *Youth Pack*, The Samaritans, Slough.

Dearling, A. & Armstrong, H. (1994) *The New Youth Games Book*, Russel House Publishing, Dorset.

DES (1967) *Children and their Primary Schools*, a Report By The Central Advisory For Education, Chaired by Lady Plowdon. HMSO, London.

DfES (1994) Circular 1/94 DfES

Douglas, T. (1983) *Group Work Practice*, Tavistock.

Duboust, S. & Knight, P. (1995) *Group Activities for Personal Development*, Speechmark, Oxford.

Dynes, R. (2001) *Anxiety Management in 10 Groupwork Sessions*, Speechmark, Oxford.

Eldridge, R. M. (1999) *Towards a Policy For Spiritual Development – A Discussion Paper*, NCC, now QCA.

Elton, Lord. (1989) *Discipline in Schools*, Report of Committee of Enquiry Chaired by Lord Elton, HMSO, London.

Fabian, H. (2000) Small Steps to Starting School. *International Journal of Early Years Education*, 8(2), 141-53.

Fuchs, B. (2002) *Group Games: Social Skills*, Speechmark, Oxford.

Galton, M., Gray, J. & Rudduck, J. (1999) *The Impact of School Transition Transfers on Pupil Progress and Attainment*, DfES Research Report No.13. DfEE, London.

Goleman, D. (1996) *Emotional Intelligence*, Bloomsbury Publishing, London.

Harvey, M. (1999) *Mind Matters: A Resource Bank on Relationships*, Youth Clubs UK, London.

Harvey, M. (2000) *Mind Matters: A Resource Bank on Actions*, Youth Clubs UK, London.

Harvey, M (2000) *Mind Matters: A Resource Bank on Self-Esteem*, Youth Clubs UK, London.

Kelly, A. (1996) *Talkabout: A Social Communication Skills Package*, Speechmark, Oxford.

Korfkamp, T. (1998) *Raising Self-Esteem and Building Self-Confidence Through Group Work*, WISARD, Wolverhampton.

Korfkamp, T. (1999) *Circle Time: A Resource Pack For Teachers and School Staff*, WISARD, Wolverhampton.

Long, R. (1999) *Exercising Self-Control*, NASEN, Wales.

Long, R. (1999) *Friendships*, NASEN, Wales.

McConnon, S. (1989) *Active Learning: A Personal Skills Course for Young People*, Macmillan Education Ltd, Surrey.

McConnon, S. (1989) *Self-Esteem: A Personal Skills Course for Young People*, Macmillan Education Ltd., Surrey.

McConnon, S. (1989) *The Nature of Friendship: A Personal Skills Course for Young People*, Macmillan Education Ltd., Surrey.

McConnon, S. (1989) *The Skills of Friendship: A Personal Skills Course for Young People*, Macmillan Education Ltd., Surrey.

McConnon, S. (1990) *Interpersonal Communication: A Personal Skills Course for Young People*, Macmillan Education Ltd., Surrey.

McConnon, S. (1992) *Feelings: A Personal Skills Course for Young People*, Macmillan Education Ltd., Surrey.

McConnon, S. (1992) *Groups: A Personal Skills Course for Young People*, Macmillan Education Ltd., Surrey.

McConnon, S. (1992) *Making Decisions: A Personal Skills Course for Young People*, Macmillan Education Ltd., Surrey.

McConnon, S. (1996) *Conflict: A Personal Skills Course for Young People*, Macmillan Education Ltd., Surrey.

Mosley, J. (1993) *Turn Your School Around*, LDA, Cambridge.

Mosley, J. & Tew, M. (1999) *Quality Circle Time in the Secondary School: A Handbook of Good Practice*, David Fulton, London.

Murphy, A. (1998) *First Lessons in Coping with Stress*, Lucky Duck Publishing Ltd., Bristol.

Myers, J. (1998) *Inside the Circle*, Special, Spring Edition.

National Healthy Schools Scheme (1999) National Healthy Schools Standard Guidance. DfEE, London.

Newton, C. & Wilson, D. (1995) *Circles of Friends*, Paper presented at EPS Nottingham.

Newton, C. & Wilson, D. (1999) *Circles of Friends*, Folens Ltd., Dunstable.

Payne, R. (2000) *Relaxation Techniques: A Practical Handbook for the Health Care Professional*, Churchill Livingstone, London.

Perry, M. & Britton, S. (1996) *How To Do Drugs: Ideas for Drug Prevention*, Hope UK, London.

Peterson, J. S. (1993) *Talk With Teens About Self and Stress*, Free Spirit, Minneapolis.

Peterson, J. S. (1993) *Talk With Teens About Feelings, Family, Relationships and the Future*, Free Spirit, Minneapolis.

Portmann, R. (2002) *Group Games: Emotional Strength and Self-Esteem*, Speechmark, Oxford.

Pru Youth Action. *Taking Action on Bullying*, Crime Concern Trust, Wiltshire.

Qualifications and Curriculum Authority (1993) *Spiritual and Moral Development – A Discussion Paper*.

Rae, T. (2000) *Confidence, Assertiveness and Self-Esteem*, Lucky Duck Publishing Ltd., Bristol.

Rae, T. (2001) *Strictly Stress: Effective Stress Management for High School Students*, Lucky Duck Publishing Ltd., Bristol.

Robinson, G. & Maines, B. (1998) *Circle Time Resources*, Lucky Duck Publishing Ltd., Bristol.

Schmuck and Schmuck (1987) In Korfkamp, T. (1998) *Raising Self-Esteem and Building Self-Confidence Through Group Work*, WISARD, Wolverhampton.

Settle, D. & Wise, C. (1986) *Choices; Materials and Methods for Personal and Social Education*, Basil Blackwell, Oxford.

Tattum, D. & Herbert, G. (1990) *Bullying: A Positive Response: Advice for parents, Governors and Staff in School*, CIHE, Cardiff.

White, M. (1999) *Magic Circles Building Self-Esteem Through Circle Time*, Lucky Duck Publishing Ltd., Bristol.

Wolverhampton Anti-Bullying Project. *A Guide for the Victims and their Families of Bullying*. WCSP and WRP, Wolverhampton.

Websites

www.bullying.co.uk

www.circletime.com

www.dfes.gov.uk

Don't forget to visit our website for all our latest publications, news and reviews.

www.luckyduck.co.uk

New publications every year on our specialist topics:

▸ **Emotional Literacy**

▸ **Self-esteem**

▸ **Bullying**

▸ **Positive Behaviour Management**

▸ **Circle Time**

▸ **Anger Management**

▸ **Asperger's Syndrome**

▸ **Eating Disorders**